Survey of Instructional Design Models

Survey of Instructional Design Models

Sixth Edition

By

Tonia A. Dousay and Robert Maribe Branch

BRILL

LEIDEN | BOSTON

Cover illustration: iStock.com/Flo

All chapters in this book have undergone peer review.

In cooperation with the Association for Educational Communications and Technology (AECT)

The Library of Congress Cataloging-in-Publication Data is available online at https://catalog.loc.gov

Typeface for the Latin, Greek, and Cyrillic scripts: "Brill". See and download: brill.com/brill-typeface.

ISBN 978-90-04-53367-7 (paperback)
ISBN 978-90-04-53368-4 (hardback)
ISBN 978-90-04-53369-1 (e-book)

Copyright 2022 by Koninklijke Brill NV, Leiden, The Netherlands.
Koninklijke Brill NV incorporates the imprints Brill, Brill Nijhoff, Brill Hotei, Brill Schöningh, Brill Fink, Brill mentis, Vandenhoeck & Ruprecht, Böhlau and V&R unipress.
All rights reserved. No part of this publication may be reproduced, translated, stored in a retrieval system, or transmitted in any form or by any means, electronic, mechanical, photocopying, recording or otherwise, without prior written permission from the publisher. Requests for re-use and/or translations must be addressed to Koninklijke Brill NV via brill.com or copyright.com.

This book is printed on acid-free paper and produced in a sustainable manner.

Contents

List of Figures VII

1 **Background of Instructional Design** 1
  1 Instructional Design Defined 2
  2 Assumptions 6

2 **Reflecting on Instructional Design** 8
  1 A Brief History 8
  2 Other Reviews 9
  3 The Role of Instructional Design Models 10
  4 Linear and Concurrent Aspects of Instructional Design 12

3 **A Taxonomy for Instructional Design Models** 13
  1 Need for an Organizing Framework 13
  2 The Taxonomy 16
  3 Delimitation 19

4 **The Models** 20
  1 The Four-Component Instructional Design (4C/ID) Model 20
  2 Agile Development Model 22
  3 The Culture Based Model 23
  4 The Dick, Carey and Carey Model 25
  5 The Gerlach and Ely Model 26
  6 The Instructional Project Development and Management (IPDM) Model 28
  7 The Interservices Procedures for Instructional Systems Development (IPISD) Model 30
  8 The ISD Model 2 32
  9 The Kemp Model 33
  10 The Layers-of-Necessity Model 35
  11 The Pebble in the Pond Model 36
  12 The Understanding by Design (UbD) Model 38

5   **Discussion**   40
     1   Scholarly Contributions   40
     2   Trends & Forecasting   41
     3   Conclusion   43

References   45
Annotated Bibliography   50

Figures

1. Core elements of instructional design.   3
2. A common portrayal of a gap analysis.   5
3. Generic portrayal of a task analysis.   5
4. A generic version of the ADDIE paradigm.   5
5. Nine events of instruction (adapted from Gagné et al., 2005, p. 30).   7
6. Rectilinear portrayal of the instructional design process.   12
7. Curvilinear portrayal of the instructional design process.   12
8. Intentional learning space.   14
9. A taxonomy for evaluating instructional design models.   16
10. The 4C/ID model (from van Merriënboer & Kirschner, 2007, p. 247).   21
11. The CBM (from Young, 2008, p. 112).   24
12. The Dick, Carey and Carey model (from Dick, Carey, & Carey, 2015, p. 1).   25
13. The Gerlach and Ely model (from Gerlach & Ely, 1980, p. 11).   27
14. The IPDM model (from Gentry, 1994, p. 1).   28
15. The IPISD model (from Branson, Rayner, Cox, Furman, & King, 1975, p. B).   30
16. The ISD model 2 (from Seels & Glasgow, 1997, p. 178).   32
17. The Kemp model (from Morrison, Ross, Morrison, & Kalman, 2019, p. 3).   34
18. The Layers-of-Necessity model (from Tessmer & Wedman, 1990, p. 79).   36
19. The Pebble in the Pond model (from Merrill, 2020, p. 166).   37

CHAPTER 1

Background of Instructional Design

This book offers a framework for exploring, adopting, or adapting instructional design (ID) models used in curriculum, course, and training development. The framework features a taxonomy that considers the prevailing teaching and learning paradigms and technology-based instructional delivery formats. The basic idea is that an instructional design process works best when matched to a corresponding context. However, educational contexts are often complex and feature compounding issues related to teaching and learning often unaccounted for during the development process. Therefore, effective instructional design models must be sensitive to different educational contexts and responsive to complex teaching and learning issues.

This edition of the *Survey of Instructional Design Models* updates and expands earlier editions by Gustafson (1981, 1991), Gustafson and Branch (1997, 2002), and Branch and Dousay (2015). Since the first appearance of instructional design (ID) models in the 1960s, many ID models have been published in instructional technology journals and other education literature. This edition presents a brief history of ID models, details a taxonomy for classifying those models, provides examples from each of the categories in the taxonomy, and describes trends in their content and focus. A list of references and a short, annotated bibliography of selected ID models complete the survey.

Only a small proportion of the available ID models were selected for this edition to illustrate the state of practice and different taxonomy categories. Choosing which models to detail was difficult since there are hundreds in the literature. Selection criteria included: historical or contemporary significance of the model, unique structure or perspective, or general distribution and citation in the literature. Due to the increasing presence of instructional design models in the literature, the review deliberately focuses on models commonly encountered in instructional design coursework and industry practice. Therefore, as a result, many excellent models are not included in this survey. Further, two new models recognize the increasing role of culture and the need for responsive design. Lastly, Cennamo and Kalk (2019) suggested that

> full-scale, systematic instructional design and development efforts are in order in at least four situations:
> – When the content is stable enough to warrant the time and costs.

- When the potential audience is large enough to warrant the time and costs.
- When communication among a team of designers and developers is required.
- When it is important to make sure that the instruction works before it's used. (p. 20)

Therefore, the models described herein generally represent the literature and contain all main concepts found in other models.

1   Instructional Design Defined

Identifying a single definition of instructional design was challenging. Although several attempts have been made to define the field and derive a standard set of meanings for various terms (Association for Educational Communications and Technology [AECT], 1977; Ely, 1973, 1983; Heinich et al., 1981; Seels & Richey, 1994), scholars have not widely adopted nor used this language consistently in the literature. For example, Seels and Richey (1994) used the term "instructional systems design" (ISD) instead of instructional development and defined it as "an organized procedure that includes the steps of analyzing, designing, developing, implementing, and evaluating instruction" (p. 31). The Seels and Richey definition is similar to how an AECT (1977) committee chaired by Kenneth Silber defined instructional development almost two decades earlier as:

> A systematic approach to the design, production, evaluation, and utilization of complete systems of instruction, including all appropriate components and a management pattern for using them; instructional development is larger than instructional product development, which is concerned with only isolated products, and is larger than instructional design, which is only one phase of instructional development. (p. 172)

Consistent with both definitions, the overall process is far more inclusive than the individual activities associated with preparing lesson specifications and determining moment-to-moment instructional strategies, sequencing, motivational elements, and students' actions.

Some educational researchers and instructional practitioners often use the terms *instructional development* and *instructional design* interchangeably and consider *instructional development* and *instructional design* as synonymous. A complete treatise on this debate is beyond the scope of this text and deserves a thorough discussion about possible differences and other nuances of each term in another forum.

Nonetheless, *instructional design* has gained dominance in the literature, so it seems prudent to use *instructional design* rather than *instructional development*. However, the fact remains that we are dealing with a comprehensive process, not one or only a few of its components. This survey uses instructional design or the acronym ID when referring to the overall process in any general narrative and actual terms when describing specific models.

Thus, it is appropriate to accept that "instructional design is a system of procedures for developing education and training materials in a consistent and reliable fashion" (Branch, 2017, p. 23). Instructional design is a complex process that promotes creativity during development and results in effective and appealing instruction for learners. Instructional design models convey guiding principles for analyzing, producing, and revising intentional learning contexts. In addition, instructional design models visually communicate their associated processes to stakeholders, illustrating the procedures that make it possible to develop effective learning designs. Figure 1 depicts the conceptual relationships among the core elements of instructional design. The five core elements (analyze, design, develop, implement, and evaluate [ADDIE]) inform each other as development progresses, and revision continues through implementation.

1.1 What's a System?

Another related term used inconsistently, further adding to the confusion of communicating the field, is *system*. The term *system* is used in at least three different ways, one of which is equivalent to how we have chosen to define instructional design. However, some authors also use the word to describe outcomes or products of a development effort. In the second perspective, the actual learner environment and related management and support components

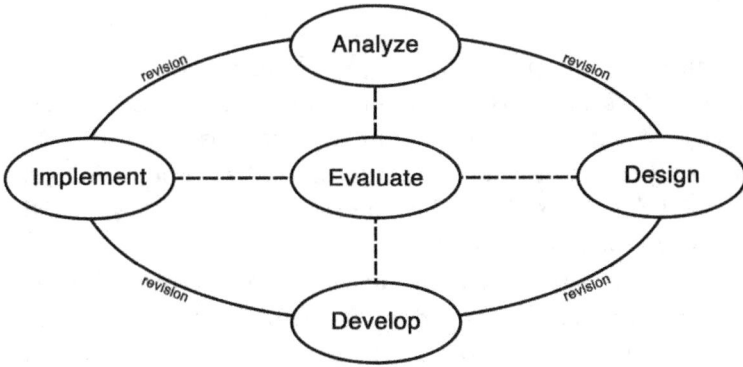

FIGURE 1   Core elements of instructional design

comprise an instructional system. A third perspective, originating in general systems theory (GST), is less commonly used. Numerous GST concepts, such as open and closed systems, entropy, and interdependence, appear in discussions about the instructional development process. In summarizing the history of instructional design, Reiser (2018) noted that:

> a variety of sets of systematic instructional design procedures (or models) have been developed, and have been referred to by such terms as the *systems approach, instructional systems design (ISD), instructional development,* and *instructional design*… Although the specific combination of procedures often varies from one instructional design model to the next, most of the models include the analysis of the instructional problems and the design, development, implementation, and evaluation of instruction procedures and materials intended to solve those problems. (p. 13)

This characterization of models as systematic emphasizes the methodological application of instructional design.

1.2 ADDIE Is a Generic Paradigm

There are many different and inconsistent uses of terminology to describe the comprehensive series of actions we call instructional design. Thus, five major activities characterize the definition of ID used in this edition:
− Analysis of the contexts and the needs of the learner,
− Design of a set of specifications for an effective, efficient, and relevant learning environment,
− Development of all student and course management materials,
− Implementation of the planned instruction, and
− Evaluation of the results of the design processes both formatively and summatively.

ADDIE describes a generic paradigm to approach instructional design. The Analyze Phase identifies the probable causes for a performance discrepancy. A *gap analysis* (Figure 2) often occurs during the Analyze Phase.

Design is typically the phase where you verify the desired performances, the learning tasks, and the appropriate testing strategies. A typical result of the Design Phase is a *task analysis* (Figure 3).

Develop refers to generating the learning resources and validating the learning resources. Implement refers to preparing the environment and other preparation required to facilitate guided learning. Lastly, evaluate refers to assessing the quality of the instruction before, during, and after implementation. Figure 4 depicts a version of the ADDIE paradigm.

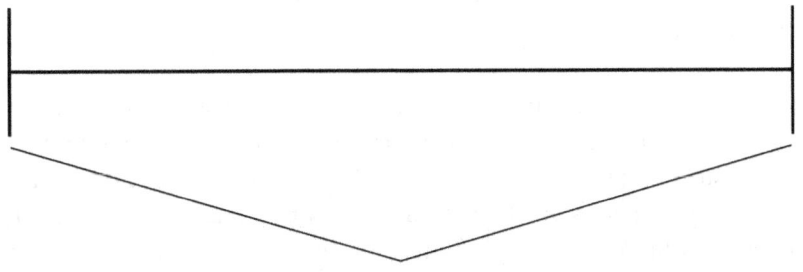

Performance Discrepancy

1. Lack of Resources (not allowed)
2. Lack of Motivation (don't want to)
3. Lack of knowledge and skill (don't know how)

FIGURE 2   A common portrayal of a gap analysis

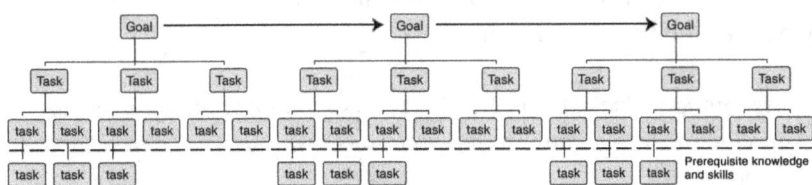

FIGURE 3   Generic portrayal of a task analysis

Analyze	Design	Develop	Implement	Evaluate
Identify performance gap	Verify desired outcomes	Generate and validate resources	Engage the students	Assess quality
1. Assess performance 2. Determine instructional goals 3. Analyze learners 4. Audit available resources 5. Determine delivery systems (including cost estimate) 6. Compose a project management plan	7. Conduct a task inventory 8. Compose performance objectives 9. Generate testing strategies 10. Calculate return on investment	11. Generate instructional strategies 12. Select or develop media 13. Develop guides for the student 14. Develop guides for the teacher 15. Conduct formative revisions 16. Conduct a Pilot Test	17. Prepare the teacher 18. Prepare the student	19. Determine evaluation criteria 20. Select evaluation tool 21. Conduct evaluation
Analysis summary	Design brief	Learning resources	Implementation strategy	Evaluation plan

FIGURE 4   A generic version of the ADDIE paradigm

The five activities in Figure 4 have often been referred to as ADDIE and labeled as a generic instructional design paradigm. The ADDIE paradigm provides a useful set of criteria for determining whether a model is inclusive of the entire ID process or focuses specifically on one or more of its elements. In some cases, designers may add a sixth activity to address monitoring distribution or monitoring of a learning environment across contexts or over an extended period. However, three assumptions are associated with adopting the ADDIE process of instructional design.

2 Assumptions

Assumptions establish baseline understandings or expectations. In research methods, assumptions provide defined parameters for accepting the suitability of data when subjecting it to analysis. Similarly, the assumptions noted present operational parameters for the design of learning. Awareness and acceptance of these assumptions benefit both long-time practitioners and those new to the field—they frame the limitations and delimitations of a systematic approach. Finally, we contend that there is ample space within the fundamental concept of instructional design to incorporate many emerging theories and philosophies of learning and advances in the technology available for design, development, and delivery of instruction. Thus, we base our definition of the process, explanation of the role of models, and the taxonomy presented for classifying them on three assumptions.

> *Assumption 1: Instructional design is a systematic process applied to develop education and training programs in a consistent and reliable fashion.*

Generally speaking, a process is any series of steps intended to reach a goal. A systematic process applies organization and logic to the steps. In ID, a systematic process aids in the decision-making process to create an intentional learning episode for education and training programs. Therefore, instructional design models customize a systematic process, attending to specific details in the learning space or context factors and elements—consistency and reliability of a process aid quality and reproducibility.

> *Assumption 2: Instructional designers apply a contextualized model while collaborating with others to create measurable learning outcomes.*

"Instructional design is a process used to generate curriculum, courses, teaching units and single episodes of guided learning" (Branch, 1999, p. 145). Instructional design models help us conceptualize the complex processes associated within a contextualized setting. Thus, an ID model requires concurrently responding to constant changes to the scope of the teaching and learning situation, generating strategies for constructing effective student-centered educational materials, and validating instructional artifacts relative to a measurable learning outcome. According to You (1993), learning is complex because knowledge is a dynamic system and an active construction of dynamic reality comprised of an interconnected web of patterns. Thus, instructional design models work best when matched to a corresponding context.

Assumption 3: Instructional design is a student-centered, responsive, generative, complex, high-fidelity, and practical process.

Facilitation and learning are inextricably connected with instruction, and you can't have one without the others. The complex nature of ID necessitates a three-component practical framework to guide application. First, facilitation is the action performed by the person or technology that directs the presentation of content and exchange of knowledge and skills. Facilitation attempts to organize external events for the purpose of constructing knowledge and skills. Second, learning is the action of an individual to construct knowledge and skills. Learning is a personal and covert cognitive activity that is distinctive to an individual. Third, instruction involves the activities between the facilitator and learners, focusing on a defined outcome.

Within this practical framework, instructional activities comprise the overt means by which knowledge, skills, and procedures are constructed during an episode of intentional learning. Effective instructional episodes have a definite beginning, middle, and end, using instructional activities to organize events that align to the defined outcome and planned assessment—demonstrating high fidelity. Many effective frameworks portray the beginning, middle, and end of instructional strategy development. However, this survey promotes an adaptation of Gagné's *Nine Events of Instruction* (Gagné et al., 2005) (Figure 5).

Lastly, instructional strategies must be student-centered, responsive, and generative. In other words, intentional learning activities should be adaptive, recognizing and respecting the positionality of learners and shifting demands on and within learning environments. However, the field could benefit from addressing ID models' accessibility and inclusivity shortcomings (Moore, 2021).

1. Gain Attention
2. Clarify Expectations
3. Review
4. Present the Content
5. Guided Practice
6. Independent Practice
7. Share New Knowledge
8. Implementation
9. Authentic Practice

FIGURE 5
Nine events of instruction (adapted from Gagné et al., 2005, p. 30)

CHAPTER 2

Reflecting on Instructional Design

1   A Brief History

Of necessity, tracing the origins of the ID model building process begins with an arbitrary date. Otherwise, we could make the case that the creators of the earliest recorded cave drawings and the scribes who produced papyrus scrolls represent the pioneers of systematic instruction. Similarly, many ideas and procedures commonly found in instructional design models, such as job analysis, measurable objectives, and performance testing, predate the period generally accepted as representing the beginnings of ID model building. Thus, instructional design requires a composite portrait to understand its foundations and identity.

The specific term *instructional development*, defined as a systematic process for improving instruction, appears to originate in a project conducted at Michigan State University from 1961–1965. The final report entitled "Instructional Systems Development: A Demonstration and Evaluation Project" (Barson, 1967) is available as an Education Resources Information Center (ERIC) document ED 020673. Set in higher education, this ID model and related project aimed to improve college courses. The Barson Model is notable in that it is one of the few models ever subjected to evaluation in a variety of projects at a variety of institutions. The Barson project also produced a set of heuristics (e.g., take faculty members out of their disciplines when showing them examples of instructional strategies) for instructional developers. These heuristics provided the basis for much of the early research on the ID process and served as a general guide for developers in higher education.

Other early works by several authors also produced ID models, although they did not use the specific term *instructional development*. The developers of programmed instruction (cf., Markle, 1964, 1978), for example, often applied a systematic process, but generally did not recognize the significant contribution of the tryout and revision process to the successes they recorded. The continued evolution of the field eventually addressed this shortsightedness.

In the 1950s and 1960s, Silvern (1965) became one of the most influential model builders. Silvern's work with the military and aerospace industry resulted in a highly complex and detailed model (with multiple variations) drawing heavily on general systems theory. The model is not widely circulated today but remains an excellent source for those willing to wade through

Silvern's sometimes obscure writing. Students of the ID process will readily see his influence on the content of contemporary models.

While at the Teaching Research Division of the Oregon State System of Higher Education, Hamreus (1967) introduced a new way of conceptualizing and implementing ID. Hamreus presented "mini" and "maxi" versions of the model, using a simple model to communicate with clients and a more detailed operational version for those working on the project. For more on Hamreus' model, see Twelker et al. (1972) for an extensive review.

Hamreus' model provided the basic structure for the Instructional Development Institute (IDI) Model (National Special Media Institute, 1971). The latter model received wide distribution, becoming among the best known in the United States in the 1970s and 1980s and forming the foundation for a five-day workshop created for teachers and administrators. By the late 1970s, more than 20,000 public school personnel had completed the workshop and used the model. In addition, graduate programs throughout the country used the workshop materials to introduce the basic concepts of the ID process. Eventually, Seels and Glasgow (1997) reproduced the IDI Model in their book, introducing it to another generation of learning designers.

2   Other Reviews

Four other major reviews of ID models frame the historical context of ID model prevalence and use. First, Stamas (1972) reviewed 23 models to determine whether or not each included a list of components he felt were part of the ID process. The AECT Division of Instructional Development reproduced this study, originally part of a Michigan State University doctoral dissertation, as an occasional paper. The dissemination of the article effectively opened the field to broader discussion and exploration.

Second, Andrews and Goodson (1980) reviewed 40 models in the *Journal of Instructional Development*. Like Stamas, Andrews and Goodson developed a matrix of ID elements and analyzed the models for their inclusion of those elements. Andrews and Goodson also attempted to trace a logical progression or evolution of later models from earlier ones but could not detect any pattern. The lack of an evolutionary pattern contributes to the general debate on the origins and scholarly merit of the field. However, such a discussion is outside the scope of this survey.

Third, Salisbury (1989) reviewed ID models appearing in major textbooks to determine the degree to which they contained specific references to general systems theory concepts. Salisbury concluded that most models contained few explicit references to those general systems concepts contained in his matrix. However, Salisbury maintained that ID is a systems discipline.

Fourth, Edmonds et al. (1994) conducted a review of ID models as a way to address proliferation over the previous decade. Edmonds et al. concluded that an ID model is better understood when classified by its context and application level for a specific context.

When considered collectively, these reviews provide an excellent sampling of the array of existing ID models and present alternate perspectives on how to examine them. It bears noting that these reviews, including up to the third edition of this survey, all concluded that the overall ID process, as initially conceived, did not change significantly despite the addition of new learning theories or design and delivery tools. However, the last few years have seen a dramatic shift in thinking about ID practice.

This transformation extends our thinking about ID rather than replacing past models and practices. Nonetheless, despite exaggerated claims of some authors at the turn of the 21st century that classic ID is dead or at least seriously ill (Gordon & Zemke, 2000), there remained considerable interest in and enthusiasm for its application (Beckschi & Doty, 2000). In fact, instructional design has emerged as one of the most popular professions in tertiary education (Berrett, 2016), especially in the wake of the COVID pandemic and increased demand for quality online learning designs (Decherney & Lavender, 2020). Instructional design models serve as conceptual, management, and communication tools for analyzing, designing, creating, and evaluating guided learning ranging from broad educational environments to narrow training applications.

3   The Role of Instructional Design Models

Consider models as a way of doing something or an explicit representation of a reality. A model can also be an example or pattern that prescribes relationships in a normative sense. Instructional design models help designers conceptualize representations of reality. In other words, a model is a simple representation of more complex forms, processes, and functions of physical phenomena or ideas. Thus, models typically seek to identify what is necessary and applicable to a context. Referring to a model when communicating with stakeholders can also aid in generating shared expectations.

An instructional design model is both descriptive and prescriptive. A visual organizer illustrates the flow of a process and demonstrates relationships between providing a rich descriptive portrait of the system. Additionally, the process is prescriptive because it guides, assigns methods and procedures, generates strategies, is goal-oriented, active, and applies a variety of models.

3.1 Conceptual Tool

Conceptual tools assist in identifying the contexts within which a designer might apply an ID model. The quantity and quality of tools accompanying a model become significant criteria for selecting one for a specific setting. In fact, both established and newer ID models accommodate emerging learning theories and a broad array of learning contexts. Philosophical orientation and theoretical perspective frame the underlying concepts of ID models, guiding a designer's decisions and conflicts. The more compatible the theory and philosophy are with the context in which a model is to be applied, the greater the potential for the model to retain its original intent and achieve fidelity among its components.

While the conceptual display of the core elements of the ID process in Figure 1 is helpful, there remains a need to indicate how to practice particular aspects of the ID process in specific contexts. It is the addition of this detail that has led to the creation of the many different models that appear in the literature. However, implementing specific procedures for planning, conducting, and managing the ID process with operational tools requires additional attention. For example, practicing IDs need project management as a competency (Ritzhaupt et al., 2021), but such detail is outside the scope of an ID model. Still, an instructional design model should contain enough information about the process to establish guidelines for managing the people, places, and things that will interact with each other and estimate the resources required to complete a project.

3.2 Operational Tool

Leveraging the conceptional into operational, models should provide a framework for selecting or constructing the functional tools needed for application. Operational tools such as program evaluation and review technique (PERT) charts, nominal group techniques, task analysis diagrams, lesson plan templates, worksheets for generating objectives, and production schedule templates actualize the ID process. Some ID models include highly prescriptive information about how to develop the companion tools or provide templates to apply the process. Other models only provide a conceptual diagram without operational tools or directions for constructing companion tools necessary.

The Interservices Procedures for Instructional Systems Development (IPISD) Model (Branson et al., 1975) represents a highly prescriptive ID model with a comprehensive set of companion operational tools. Similarly, the Dick, Carey and Carey model (2015) is moderately prescriptive and contains many companion operational tools. By contrast, Zemke and Kramlinger (1982) and Gentry (1994) provide few or no accompanying tools, describing appropriate tools instead. Generic operational tools for managing ID (e.g., Greer, 1992) also are available.

4 Linear and Concurrent Aspects of Instructional Design

The instructional design process can be approached as a single linear process or as a set of concurrent or recursive procedures. Instructional design should be portrayed in ways that communicate the true richness and reality associated with planning instruction. Critics of ID models sometimes interpret them as stifling, passive, lockstep, and simple because of the visual elements used to compose the model (Branch, 1997). This perception arises partially because ID models traditionally present as rectilinear rows of boxes connected by straight lines with one-way arrows and one or more feedback (revision) lines parallel to other straight lines (Figure 6).

Rectilinear portrayals of ID models often do not acknowledge the actual complexities of the instructional development process. Curvilinear compositions of ovals connected by curved lines with two-way arrows better acknowledge the complex reality upon which the ID process is modeled (Figure 7). However, an implied sequence remains, at least among the core elements. The depiction of a model influences its interpretation (Branch et al., 2018), a limitation of note when communicating with stakeholders.

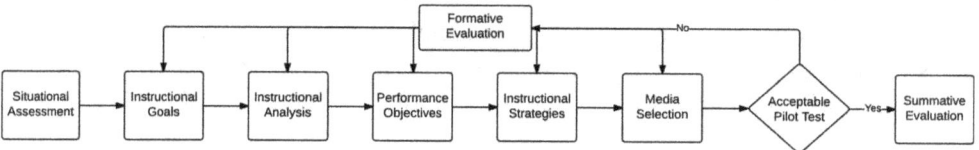

FIGURE 6 Rectilinear portrayal of the instructional design process

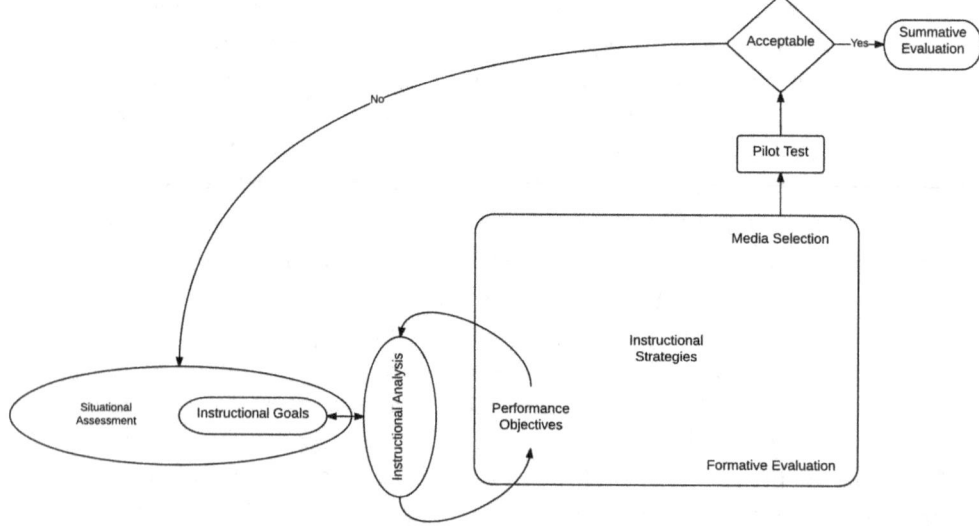

FIGURE 7 Curvilinear portrayal of the instructional design process

CHAPTER 3

A Taxonomy for Instructional Design Models

This chapter offers a taxonomy for identifying an instructional design model appropriate for a defined teaching and learning context. Referencing such a tool is particularly important for the varied digital learning environments that have emerged and continue to evolve in modern society. The ubiquitous nature of digital access, applications, and resources situates an increasing proportion of contemporary learning experiences in unique learning spaces. Thus, trends associated with mobile communication devices, social media platforms, artificial intelligence, robotics, learning management systems, micro-computing technologies, remote learning situations, access to real-time data, gaming and gamification, virtual reality, and augmented reality contribute to the complex structure of designing learning. Therefore, instructional design models must be capable of accommodating uncommon learning spaces and innovative teaching and learning strategies.

1 Need for an Organizing Framework

Instructional design models vary widely in their purposes; the amount of detail provided; the degree of application linearity; and the quantity, quality, and utility of the accompanying operational tools. While no single model is useful for all settings and purposes, it is important to identify the intended focus of an ID model and its intended context. The taxonomy of ID models can help guide adopting or adapting instructional design models. The following questions may help designers critically evaluate models:
- What are the underlying assumptions of this model?
- What learning space components apply to the current project?
- What factors of this model correlate to conditions of the project's context?
- How does the current project differ from the model's guidance?
- What other aspects of the taxonomy guide applicability or fit of this model?

1.1 *A Response to the Complexity of Intentional Learning*
Student-centered spaces, wherever located, represent an epistemological shift from regarding students as the occupants of learning spaces to regarding students' actions during guided learning as the motivation for the design

of instruction. Thus, a clear understanding of the complexities of intentional learning warrants attention.

Complexity is common in biological organisms, geological formations, and social constructions, such as education. Educational researchers and practitioners routinely encounter complex situations as a function of study and practice. Managing complex situations have become an everyday necessity for instructional designers and developers to make sense of complicated situations, such as those that occur in the classroom.

Indeed, emerging philosophies about instruction, education, and learning theories re-focus the *classroom* concept to include a broader array of contexts. While classrooms are defined as 'a place where classes meet,' the prevailing societal paradigm typically shapes classrooms. Until recently, classrooms replicated our desire to compartmentalize, consistent with the industrial age. The desire to regiment and control was reflected in classrooms patterned after military models, but classrooms are beginning to reflect a societal shift to an information age.

Classrooms of the information age can be situated at remote sites, accessed at convenient times, and personalized to match the capability of individual learners. While students may still 'meet' to study the same subject, the location, time, and pace are now dynamic. Educators and trainers should regard a classroom as any potential learning space. While each episode of intentional learning is distinctive and separate, each remains part of a larger curricular scheme. Episodes of guided learning are characterized by several participating entities which are themselves complex: the learner, the content, the media, the teacher, peers, and the context, all interacting within a discrete period while moving toward a common goal (Figure 8).

Learning refers to the process of acquiring knowledge and skill. Intentional learning refers to learning that happens through purposefully arranged

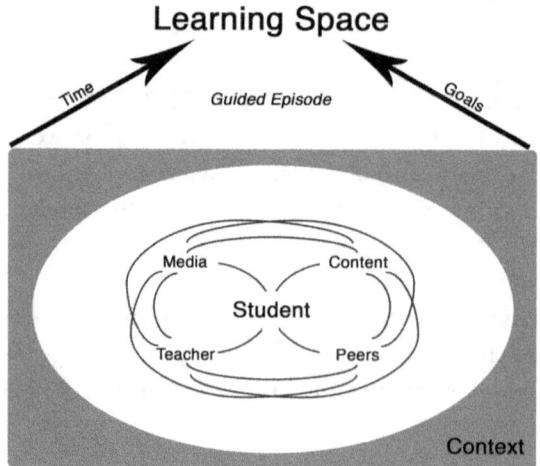

FIGURE 8
Intentional learning space

information, human resources, and environments to achieve a specific purpose. Intentional learning is complex because of the nature of knowledge and nonlinear interactions among multiple entities. Branch (1999) identified eight elements always present within an intentional learning space: student, content, media, teacher, peers, time, goal, and context.

Branch purported that each of these eight elements is inherently complex. The student is complex because of human beings' physical, emotional, social, and mental development and the effect of intelligence, cognitive styles, motivation, cultural norms, creativity, and socio-economic status on behavior patterns. Content is complex because it is a collection of concepts, rules, propositions, procedures, and socially constructed information. Moreover, the information types may be attributes, categorical, classification, component parts, dimension, elaboration, goal, hierarchy, kinds, matrix, prerequisite, procedural, rule, skills, and type. A peer is a complex entity because of all the social negotiations among persons of the same age, status, or ability. Media are channels of communication that come in a multitude of forms. The facilitator, or facilitator function, assumes the executive decision-making role, such as identifying appropriate goals and expectations, analyzing learning needs, arranging content information, choosing media, selecting instructional methods, and conducting assessments on instruction and students. Time is a complex entity because it is omnipresent and is measurable by assigning discrete increments and intervals but not controlled. Context is the complex entity that refers to those conditions that directly and indirectly influence situations, environments, and communities. Contextual conditions are formed by physical, political, economic, and cultural settings: human ecology. Instructional development models provide conceptual tools for responding to the complexity of intentional learning.

1.1.1 Contextualizing the Learning Space

Rather than defining context, this taxonomy characterizes context as encompassing three factors: scope of practice, learning strategy, and reality trait. Specific elements of each contextual factor establish needs and constraints. Thus, the taxonomy delineates the scope of practice in terms of opportunity for conducting an analysis, functional specifications by design, depth of development, resources required for implementation, and cycles of formative evaluation. Similarly, the taxonomy delineates learning strategy in terms of types of instructional strategies, such as case-based learning, problem-based learning, project-based learning, active learning, action learning, and experiential learning. Finally, the taxonomy delineates the situation's reality in terms of learner-centered traits, conceptual period of time, access to real-time data, authenticity, genuineness, and augmentation. Shared or similar elements form the foundation for classifying and considering instructional design model suitability and applicability.

Lastly, additional operational variables characterize intentional learning spaces. For example, issues such as resources committed to the development effort, whether it is a team or individual effort, expected instructional design skill and experience of the individual or team, whether most instructional materials would be selected from existing sources or represent original design and production, amount of needs analysis conducted, the anticipated technological complexity of the development and delivery environments, amount of dissemination and follow-up occurring after development. These variables enable instructional designers to apply models that facilitate contextualized, multi-functional, ill-structured, practical, and inspirational learning spaces.

2 The Taxonomy

The current taxonomy recognizes contemporary instructional delivery formats and identifies common factors and elements commensurate with current instructional design industry standards. Figure 9 depicts a matrix relating the

		Taxonomy	
Learning Space	In-Person	Same physical space and same time	
	Virtual	Synchronous = any place, but same time	
		Asynchronous = any place and any time	
	Hybrid	Combination of In-person and Virtual	
	Factor	**Elements**	
Context	1. Scope of Practice	a. Opportunity for conducting an **Analysis** b. Functional specifications by **Design** c. Depth of **Development** d. Resources required for **Implementation** e. Cycles of formative **Evaluation**	
	2. Learning Strategy	a. Case-based learning b. Problem-based learning c. Project-based learning d. Active learning e. Action learning f. Experiential learning	
	3. Reality Trait	a. Learner-centered b. Defined period of time c. Accesses real-time data d. Authentic e. Genuine f. Augmented	

FIGURE 9   A taxonomy for evaluating instructional design models

type of learning space (in-person, virtual, hybrid) to contextual factors (scope of practice, learning strategy, reality trait). The matrix categorizes common teaching and learning modalities, factors, and elements to aid with selecting or tailoring an instructional design model to fit learning space and contextual needs.

2.1 Who Is the Primary Audience for the Taxonomy?

The taxonomy should benefit anyone interested in instructional design, meaning those at practically any level of prior knowledge about the systematic design of instruction. However, the taxonomy is likely to be most useful to people at the ends of the instructional design knowledge continuum: novice instructional designers on one end and instructional design scholars on the other end. Novice instructional designers should find the taxonomy a helpful tool for critically reflecting on design elements and comparing one instructional design model to another. Instructional design scholars should find value in highlighting foundational attributes as they consider the validity of an instructional design model. Finally, learning professionals who consider themselves at other points along the instructional design knowledge continuum might view the taxonomy as a starting point for ways to think about instructional design models and practice.

2.2 What Type of Models Are Categorized in the Taxonomy?

This survey features models that embody a product development process. The products are tools and processes used to create effective teaching and learning materials. Previous versions of the taxonomy categorized models as classroom-, product-, or system-oriented. While these three classifications remain a valid consideration, especially when considering the complexity of a product, the current taxonomy enhances the depth of treatment regarding the selected characteristics of instructional design models to be more inclusive of the varying contexts and products that support teaching and learning.

2.3 When Should the Taxonomy Be Used?

The taxonomy applies to all formal processes of systematically developing instructional materials. Formal, systematic processes include the planning phase of a project to develop teaching and learning materials before finalizing a scope of work. The taxonomy is also useful during a team's initial development stage, where the purpose is to build community around the process that will be adopted for moving forward with a defined learning project. In addition, the taxonomy also proves helpful for managing client expectations about the activities and results of an instructional design process.

The taxonomy is intended to help designers consider the characteristics of a design context and select a specific model or suitable aspects of different models. An example is when a learning context limits the opportunity for formative evaluation or when user feedback is needed frequently; an instructional designer may benefit from employing different models' elements associated with the *Scope of Practice*. In the example above, designers may benefit from incorporating the evaluative elements of rectilinear models when the content is relatively stable, or the intended audience is comparatively large. Considering the type of learning spaces and contextual factors noted in the taxonomy empowers instructional designers to make informed decisions about the models they use and the reasons for doing so.

2.4   Where Should the Taxonomy Be Used?

The reality of practicing instructional design in a variety of contexts contributes directly to the copious number of models created to reflect these variations. Taxonomies are useful because they can clarify underlying assumptions and help identify the conditions for selecting a model best matched to a defined context.

2.5   Why Should Instructional Designers Use a Taxonomy?

Over the years, the taxonomy has proven an excellent reference for learning professionals who need to craft events of instruction vis-à-vis the systematic development of effective teaching materials. The revised taxonomy pays respect to the nuanced nature of learning spaces in the 21st century and the diverse learning that occurs through these spaces. Further, instructional design scholars may find the taxonomy instrumental in organizing the extensive literature about instructional design models, critically evaluating an instructional design model, or validating a new model.

2.6   How Should the Taxonomy Be Used?

The concept that comes to mind is the *Law of Requisite Variety* (Ashby, 1957). The contention here is that instructional design contexts represent a variety of states that are diverse, active, creative, iterative, and complex. Thus, an instructional design model must be sufficiently complex to address the degree of complexity inherent in the context of its application. This central idea is consistent with Ashby's notion that "If a system is to be stable, the number of states of its control mechanism must be greater than or equal to the number of states in the system being controlled." The rationale for using the taxonomy stems from the need to match the complexity of an end result, such as goals and objectives, with the complexity of the procedures required to maintain consistency and reliability throughout a defined process, such as instructional design.

3 Delimitation

Instructional design is practiced in a variety of settings, leading to the creation of many different models. While published instructional design models number in the dozens, they typically have categorical differences. The significant differences often address the type of learning, expected outcome or use, and other considerations affecting the contextual relevance of an instructional design model. Thus, there is value in creating a taxonomy for matching an instructional design model to an appropriate context. The taxonomy presented in this edition of the *Survey of Instructional Design Models* revises the characteristics identified in the taxonomies of Gustafson (1981), Gustafson and Branch (2002), and Branch and Dousay (2015). As discussed earlier, three assumptions underlie the current taxonomy:
- Instructional design is a systematic process applied to develop education and training programs consistently and reliably.
- Instructional designers apply a contextualized model while collaborating with others to create measurable learning outcomes.
- Instructional design is a student-centered, responsive, generative, complex, high-fidelity, and practical process.

CHAPTER 4

The Models

We believe that these models serve as conceptual and communication tools to visualize, direct, and manage processes for creating high-quality instruction. Seel (1997) identified three types of ID models (theoretical/conceptual, organization, and planning-and-prognosis) and would label those we review here as organization models, useful as general prescriptions for instructional planning. Models also assist us in selecting or developing appropriate operational tools and techniques through application. Finally, models serve as a source of research questions as we revisit existing learning theories and investigate emerging theories related to learning development.

However, models are rarely tested in the sense of rigorous assessment, and one should not conflate evaluation with research. Indeed, evaluation tests a model's application and resulting instruction against predetermined criteria or other defined processes. Instead, ID models with wide distribution and acceptance gain their credibility by being found useful by practitioners, who frequently adapt and modify them to match specific conditions.

1 The Four-Component Instructional Design (4C/ID) Model

Originally developed by Jeroen van Merriënboer, the Four-Component Instructional Design (4C/ID) model proposes a holistic design approach in contrast to traditional fragmented methods prescribed by most instructional design models (van Merriënboer & Kirschner, 2007). The 4C/ID model aims to integrate declarative, procedural, and affective learning in a coalesced knowledge base rather than focusing on compartmentalizing each domain. Designers follow ten steps divided among the four components to enact this approach:

1. Learning Tasks
   – Design learning tasks
   – Sequence task classes
   – Set performance objectives
2. Supportive Information
   – Design supportive information
   – Analyze cognitive strategies
   – Analyze mental models

3. Procedural Information
   - Design procedural information
   - Analyze cognitive rules
   - Analyze prerequisite knowledge
4. Part-task Practice
   - Design part-task practice

The 4C/ID Model assumes that these four components and ten steps are blueprints for complex learning. Designers must initially define what occurs within each area to understand the model's components better. First, "learning tasks" must be authentic, whole-task experiences based on real-life tasks that focus on integrating skills, knowledge, and attitudes. In Figure 10, the blueprint circles represent "learning tasks." Second, the model recognizes any helpful resource that assists learning, problem-solving, and reasoning as "supportive information." The blueprint's wide bars beneath and between learning tasks depict "supportive information." Third, the "procedural information"

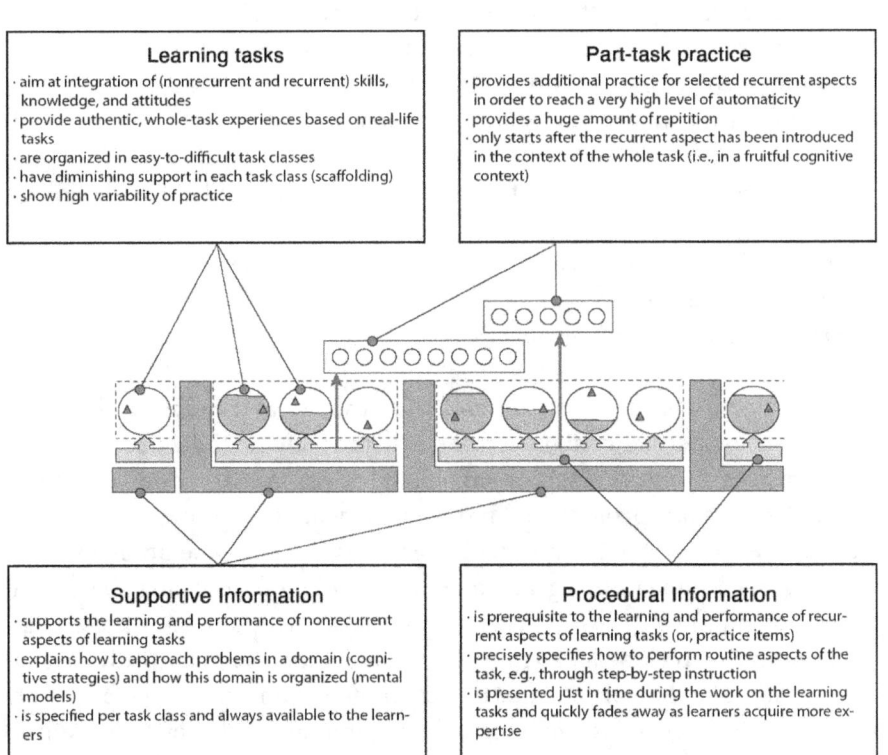

FIGURE 10   The 4C/ID model (from van Merriënboer & Kirschner, 2007, p. 247)

component includes all prerequisite knowledge and skill necessary for each "learning task." The thin bars between learning tasks and supportive information represent procedural information. Lastly, the model prescribes practice items to help learners reach a high level of automaticity for routine aspects of a "learning task" and refers to these as "part-task practice." The smaller circles with a bar depict "part-task practice" components in the blueprint.

Overall, the 4C/ID model provides a unique approach to designing instructional experiences. However, the focus is on designing and developing instruction with no discussion on activating or evaluating and revising instruction.

2 Agile Development Model

The Agile development model is commonly recognized and used by software developers. Created as a manifesto written by 17 software developers (Beck et al., 2001), the Agile approach promotes:
- Individuals and interactions over processes and tools
- Working software over comprehensive documentation
- Customer collaboration over contract negotiation
- Responding to change over following a plan

Furthermore, practitioners of Agile appreciate the model's methodology, which is:
- Empirical (learn the process)
- Iterative (small steps)
- Participatory (frequent feedback)

Instructional designers in international business and industry choose to adopt Agile for instructional processes due to the focus on individuals and outcomes instead of following a prescribed, linear plan. In addition, the model emphasizes self-organization and motivation, facilitating continuous collaboration between stakeholders and developers. This latter consideration responds to the challenge of identifying all requirements during the opening phase of an instructional project. Thus, it becomes crucial to incorporate modes of communication that include all team members and a representative of the stakeholder. The Agile Model refers to this communication specifically as a daily scrum meeting, which lasts no longer than 15 minutes and allows all involved parties to report on the previous day's development activities, indicate the next course of action, and identify any issues or problems that are prohibiting progress. The primary measure of progress in the model is a working product.

Instructional designers using Agile benefit from the model's inherent flexibility. The focus on individuals and interactions allows team members to draw upon whatever tools or processes fit the specific project's needs. Designers can also devote development time and resources to the end product(s) instead of writing supplemental or completing documentation. As implied by the name, the model promotes agility by allowing designers and developers to adjust the development plan in progress when encountering a significant issue or problem. The daily reporting mechanism of the Agile process affords a clear, continuous understanding by all parties and expedites the overall process.

However, the strength of the Agile Model hinges on team composition and the relationship between designers and stakeholders. Communication processes may degrade or break down quickly when accommodating multiple external factors, such as stakeholder representative(s), developers, subject matter experts, etc. Agile may work well for instructional designers who work on software-related projects, where the process is familiar to stakeholders, and large name software corporations advocate for using Agile.

3 The Culture Based Model

A newcomer to this survey, Young (2008) examined two decades of literature investigating models of culture in ID to "guide the design of culture-based products and services, and foster cross-cultural communications, relations, and meanings" (p. 107). This labor yielded the Culture Based Model (CBM), a framework with eight focus areas to guide function and selection processes iteratively. Each of the eight areas (Figure 11) contains as few as three or as many as 25 design factors. Each design factor, 70 in total, serves a different function, and questions designers ask about each factor help frame their resulting action in a culturally responsive way.

Young's (2008) systematically qualitative approach to generating the CBM addresses a much-needed area of ID design, focusing on less visible learner needs. Three African American instructional products created over the course of 100 years anchor a historical analysis to "find culture." The author conducted context and text analyses of cultural remnants within each product. The resulting findings translate into the CBM, serving as relevant design factors. For example, the second instructional product analyzed connects to the model's Inquiry area, where the subsequent design factors include visual representations, and more specifically, designer questions such as how do the visual representations frame the product? and who is portrayed in these visual representations?

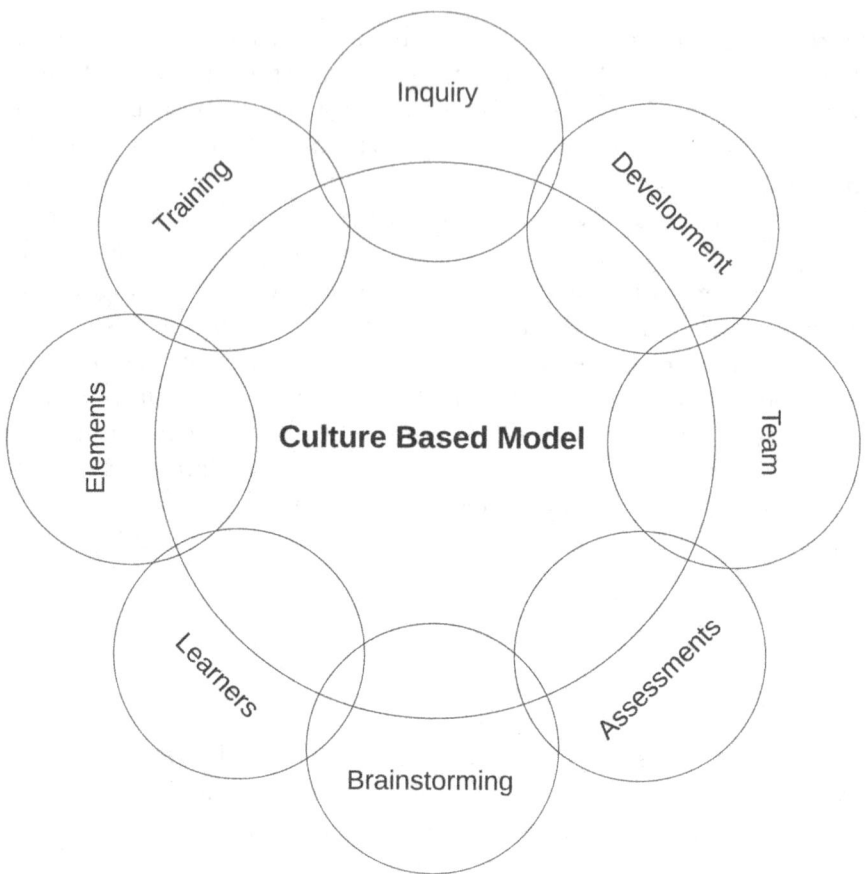

FIGURE 11   The CBM (from Young, 2008, p. 112)

The CBM treats ID as a project to manage, similar to the ISD Model 2, dividing the project into eight areas. These areas include "Inquiry" (monitoring project design), "Development" (problem-solving for project management), "Team" (decision making for project management), "Assessments" (evaluation during project management), "Brainstorming" (planning during project management), "Learners" (learning aspects), "Elements" (content development), and "Training" (implementation support).

The detailed nature of each area's definition, function, and overview of relevant design factors prevents a comprehensive summary, but two factors deserve special recognition. First, within the area of "Development," the CBM challenges designers to explore individual and group environmental cultures, including workplace, community, or school culture, and these influences on learning design. Second, designers seeking to integrate culturally relevant decision-making should attend to the "Elements" area, in which Young further divides the area into three sections: "Anthropology of Culture," "Psychology of Culture," and "Science of Culture." These sections further delve into tangible and intangible design factors, such as cultural communication, ways of knowing, identity, futures, and more. Designers looking to adopt or adapt the CBM to meet the needs of culturally diverse learners will appreciate how the design factors within each area align to elements of the taxonomy, especially reality traits.

4   The Dick, Carey and Carey Model

Without a doubt, the most widely cited ID model is the one initially published by Walter Dick and Lou Carey to which they added James Carey. Both advocates of ID and its most vocal critics almost invariably cite this model when expressing their opinions about the desirability of systematically designing instruction. Moreover, the Dick, Carey and Carey model has become the standard by which the field compares all other ID models (and alternative approaches to design and development of instruction). Hence, its selection again for inclusion in this publication. This model is flexible for different learning spaces and elements, defining the size and scope in the first step ("Identify Instructional Goals").

In this widely used text, now in its eighth edition (Dick et al., 2015), the model (Figure 12) is mostly unchanged from earlier editions. The authors focused this update on attending to the increased role of portable digital devices as a common delivery mechanism and the alignment between assessment and authentic performance. The authors also provide a second case study in the Appendices in addition to the serial case present throughout the text. In the context of previous surveys, we consider the model well-suited for a course or system-level project.

Dick, Carey and Carey's model begins with "Identify Instructional Goal(s)." The first component of their model immediately distinguishes it from many

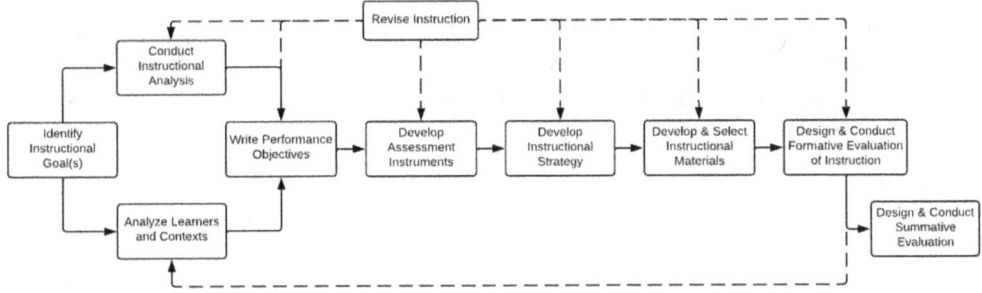

FIGURE 12   The Dick, Carey and Carey model (from Dick, Carey, & Carey, 2015, p. 1)

other instructional development models by promoting needs assessment procedures and the importance of identifying clear and measurable goals. The authors recommend criteria for establishing instructional goals to decide what you are trying to achieve before beginning the ID process. Next, designers use two steps in parallel, "Conduct Instructional Analysis" and "Analyze Learners and Contexts," to oversee a comprehensive analysis. The former is a vintage hierarchical analysis as conceived by Gagné, with added procedures for constructing cluster analysis diagrams for verbal information. The latter step specifies collecting information about prospective learners' knowledge, skills and attitudes, and learning environment.

Designers next "Write Performance Objectives" in measurable terms, followed by "Developing Assessment Instruments." These traditional assessments generate criterion-referenced test items for each objective. Next, in the "Develop Instructional Strategy" step, the authors recommend ways to develop strategies for assisting a particular group of learners in achieving the stated objectives. The next step is to "Develop and Select Instructional Materials." Dick, Carey, and Carey acknowledge the desirability of selecting and developing materials, but the degree of emphasis devoted to development suggests they are far more interested in original content.

The next step is to "Design and Conduct Formative Evaluation," a process for which they give excellent guidance. Conducting a formative evaluation of instructional materials is iterative and consists of at least three data collection cycles, analysis, and revision. The first cycle pinpoints errors in the materials. The second cycle occurs after these errors have been corrected and is designed to locate additional errors in the materials and procedures. The third cycle is a field trial conducted following the refinement of materials after the second cycle. It is intended to identify errors when the materials are used in their intended setting. Finally, "Design and Conduct Summative Evaluation" also determines the degree to which the original instructional goals (and perhaps other unintended ones) have been achieved.

The Dick, Carey and Carey model reflects the fundamental design process used in many business, industry, government, and military training settings and the influence of performance technology and the application of computers to instruction. It is remarkably detailed and helpful during the analysis and evaluation phases of a project.

5   The Gerlach and Ely Model

The Gerlach and Ely (1980) model combines linear and concurrent development activities (Figure 13). Although multiple phases facilitate simultaneous steps,

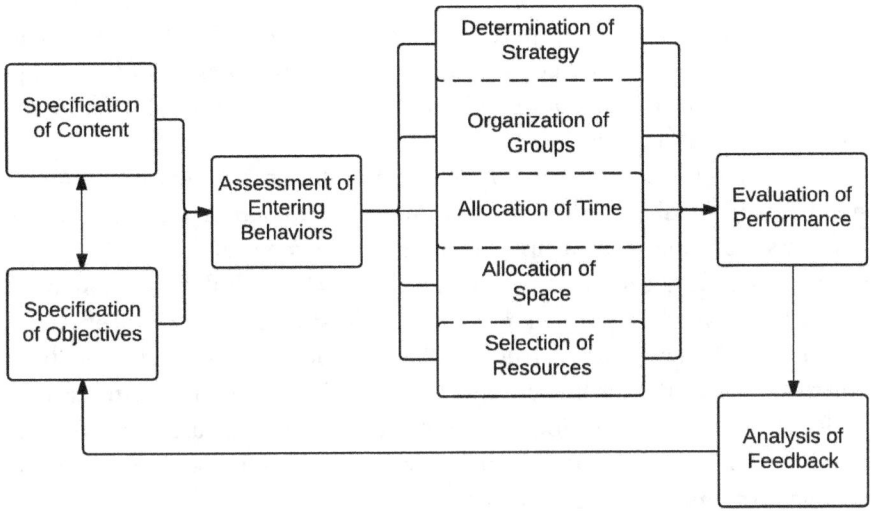

FIGURE 13   The Gerlach and Ely model (from Gerlach & Ely, 1980, p. 11)

the overall model portrays a linear orientation. The entry point of the model calls for identifying content and specifying objectives as concurrent, interactive activities. While Gerlach and Ely prefer specifying objectives as a "first task," they recognize that many teachers first think about content, making this model one of the few with such a distinction. The model prescribes writing and classifying learning objectives before making several design decisions. The classification scheme is based on Gerlach's other scholarly work and presents a five-part cognitive taxonomy with single categories for affective and motor skill objectives.

The second phase in Gerlach and Ely's model assesses learners' entry behavior, a step common to many classroom-oriented models. In the third phase, five concurrent activities guide learning design. The authors view these activities as interactive, with any decision in one area influencing the range of decisions available in the others. The five activities are: (1) determine strategy, (2) organize groups, (3) allocate time, (4) allocate space, and (5) select resources.

Under strategies, the authors posit a continuum from exposition- (all cues) to discovery-learning (no cues). The designer's role is to select one or more strategies along this continuum. Similarly, the authors recommend organizing students into configurations ranging from self-study to whole-class activities based on activities, space, time, and resources. Gerlach and Ely view time as a constant divided up among various strategies. Space is not a constant because teachers can and should extend learning experiences beyond the classroom, which itself can be rearranged for different grouping patterns.

The selection of resources focuses on the designer's need to locate, obtain, and adapt or supplement existing instructional materials. The model emphasizes where and how to find such resources and the importance of previewing and planning their use as a part of the overall instructional strategy. This emphasis on selecting rather than developing instructional materials supports instructional design common in traditional PK-12 classrooms where the designer is often the teacher.

Gerlach and Ely close out the model with evaluating student performance and analyzing feedback to inform revisions. The evaluation phase directs the designer's attention to measuring learner achievement and attitude toward the content and instruction. The designer should closely link evaluation to the learner objectives with particular attention to examining the overall effectiveness and efficiency of the instruction. The last phase incorporates feedback from the evaluation regarding the effectiveness of the instruction with the possibility of making revisions for future delivery. Feedback focuses on reviewing all earlier steps in the model, emphasizing reexamining decisions regarding the objectives and strategies selected.

6   The Instructional Project Development and Management (IPDM) Model

Gentry (1994) created the Instructional Project Development and Management (IPDM) model intending to integrate both the concepts and procedures of ID and supporting processes (Figure 14). The IPDM model attends to 13 total components and how to complete each during an instructional development project, including multiple techniques and job aids to support this work. According to Gentry, the IPDM model is suited for graduate students, practicing instructional designers, and teachers. However, the comprehensive description of the entire process and the accompanying tools for managing large projects also make it suitable for developing large-scale systems.

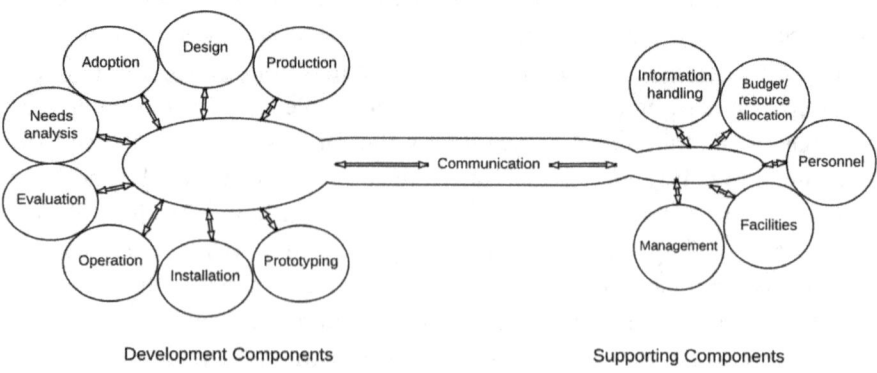

FIGURE 14   The IPDM model (from Gentry, 1994, p. 1)

Gentry divided the IPDM model into two groups: Development Components and Supporting Components, with a Communication mechanism connecting the two clusters. There are eight development components: (1) Needs Analysis (establish needs and prioritize goals for existing or proposed instruction); (2) Adoption (establish acceptance by decision-makers, and obtain commitment of resources); (3) Design (specify objectives, strategies, techniques, and media); (4) Production (construct project elements specified by the design and revision data); (5) Prototyping (assemble, pilot test, validate, and finalize an instructional unit); (6) Installation (establish the necessary conditions for effective operation of a new instructional product), (7) Operation (maintaining the instructional product after its installation); and (8) Evaluation (collect, analyze, and summarize data to enable revision decisions).

There are five supporting processes: (1) Management (process by which resources are controlled, coordinated, integrated, and allocated to accomplish project goals); (2) Information Handling (process of selecting, collecting, generating, organizing, storing, retrieving, distributing, and assessing information required by an ID project); (3) Resource Acquisition and Allocation (processes for determining resource needs, formalizing budgets, and acquiring and distributing resources); (4) Personnel (processes for determining staffing needs, hiring, training, assessing, motivating, counseling, censuring, and dismissing ID project members); and (5) Facilities (process for organizing and renovating spaces for design, implementation, and testing of elements of instruction).

The IPDM model emphasizes the importance of sharing information between the two clusters of components during the life of the instructional development project. The communication component is the "process by which essential information is distributed and circulated among those responsible for, or involved in, the activities of a project" (Gentry, 1994, p. 5).

Fang and Strobel (2001) adapted the IPDM model for use in game design. Applying Gentry's model in this context provided a constructivist learning environment. Specifically, the use of the model in a game design context served as process scaffolding and was well received by novice designers. As a result, it may be worthwhile to consider applying IPDM to different learning contexts with varying taxonomy factors and elements.

The IPDM model's unique quality is how the instructional development process relates to specific implementation techniques. Some designers view the model as a mechanistic approach to instructional development because it relies on jargon and a behavioristic orientation. However, Gentry warns against being overly dogmatic and linear in applying his model. The model depicts procedures that contain enough descriptive and prescriptive information and at varying levels of detail, to make it a comprehensive introduction to the processes and techniques of instructional development.

7 The Interservices Procedures for Instructional Systems Development (IPISD) Model

The Interservices Procedures for Instructional Systems Development (IPISD) model was, as the name suggests, a joint effort of the United States military services. The Army, Navy, Marines, and Air Force created this model (Figure 15) to produce a common rigorous procedure for developing effective instruction. In addition, the developers felt that a shared development model would improve communication with contractors developing instruction across different branches of the military. Many personnel contributed to creating the IPISD model; however, the name most commonly associated with it is Robert Branson.

The IPISD model has several layers of detail. The model contains five phases: Analyze, Design, Develop, Implement, and Control. These phases sub-divide into 20 steps, which can be further divided into hundreds of sub-steps. We note that the IPISD model is one of the most highly detailed models of the

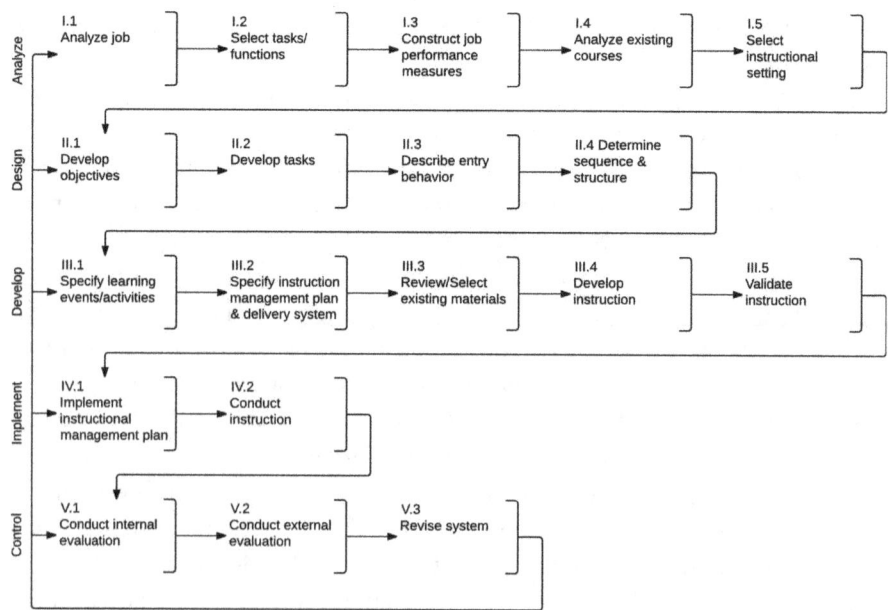

FIGURE 15   The IPISD model (from Branson, Rayner, Cox, Furman, & King, 1975, p. B)

ID process generally available, published as a four-volume set (Branson et al., 1975) and available from the National Technical Information Service (NTIS) via ERIC.

A detailed review of all the steps in this model is beyond the scope of this survey. Thus, this summary only addresses the phase level. Recall that the IPISD model is designed specifically for military training. Most other models have a much broader range of intended applications. The narrower focus of IPISD is both a blessing and a bane. Its virtue is the highly detailed level of specification it contains. However, the price of this specification is the lack of generalizability of many of its specific procedures to other contexts.

Phase one of IPISD (analyze) requires specification of the tasks military personnel perform on the job. First, tasks that are already known or easy to acquire are subtracted, generating a list of tasks requiring instruction. Next, designers specify performance levels and evaluation procedures for the tasks, examining existing courses for applicability. The designer then decides to modify the existing course to fulfill task requirements or plan a new course. The final step in phase one is to determine the most appropriate site for instruction; i.e., school or non-resident instruction.

Phase two (design) begins with arranging job tasks into instructional outcomes classified by the learning elements involved. Next, designers generate and validate tests on a population sample and write instructional objectives in behavioral form. Then, the designer determines the entry behavior expected of typical students, followed by ordering the sequence and structure for the course.

The development of prototype materials occurs in phase three of the model. Development begins with specifying a list of events and activities for inclusion in instruction. Designers then select media and develop a course management plan. This phase includes reviewing existing instructional materials for relevance and, if appropriate, adopting or adapting for the course. Lastly, designers produce new materials and facilitate field-testing the entire package for revisions until achieving satisfactory learner and system performance.

Phase four (implement) includes training course managers in using the package and subject matter personnel to manage or deliver the training as well as distributing all materials to the selected sites. This phase includes conducting the instruction and collecting evaluation data on the learners and system performance.

During phase five (control), "on-line staff" perform an internal evaluation, making small-scale changes to improve the system after each offering. In addition, the staff forward evaluation results to a central location. Then, an external evaluation team identifies significant deficiencies requiring immediate correction. The external evaluation also follows course graduates to the job site to assess real-world performance and monitors changes in field practices to determine necessary course revisions. Thus, phase five emphasizes quality control and the continued relevance of the training over an extended period.

The primary strength of the IPISD model is the extensive specification of procedures to follow during the ID process. Its significant limitations are the narrow instructional focus and linear approach to ID. Interested designers should refer to Berkowitz and O'Neil's (1979) annotated bibliography of relevant resources for the IPISD model.

8 The ISD Model 2

In the second edition of their book Seels and Glasgow (1997) presented the "ISD model 2: for Practitioners" (Figure 16). The authors compared their model to others and the generic ADDIE process, concluding it is similar to many others but assumes a project management positionality. Thus, they organize the model into three management phases: problem analysis management, instructional design management, and implementation and evaluation management.

The ultimate diffusion of learning products and their adoption cuts across all three phases. This emphasis recognizes problems often encountered by developers who fail to consider how diffusion and adoption will occur until the end, resulting in unsatisfied clients and users or minimal adoption. Seels and Glasgow provide specifics on conducting each phase, including related exercises for each step. The steps within each phase may be performed linearly but

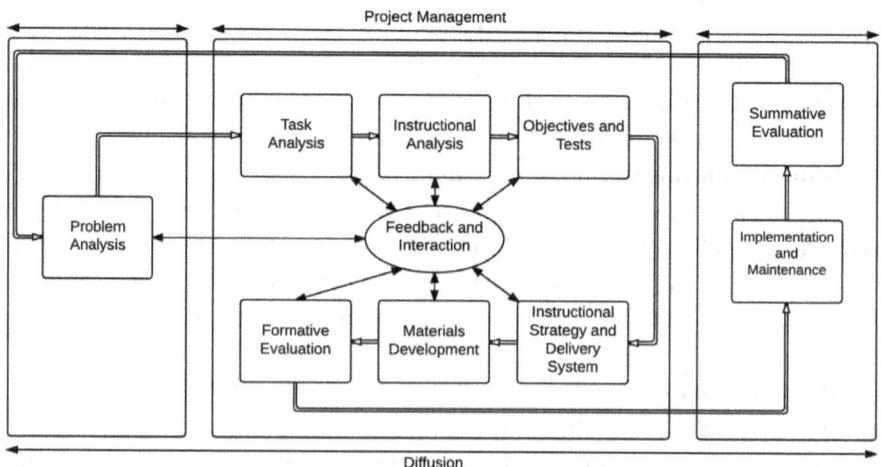

FIGURE 16   The ISD model 2 (from Seels & Glasgow, 1997, p. 178)

often are not, although the three phases are generally considered self-contained and linear. Further, the authors assert that the instructional design phase steps are interdependent and concurrent and may involve iterative cycling.

The first phase of project management, problem analysis, involves all the decisions associated with conducting needs analysis and formulating a management plan. These decisions include "needs assessment (goals), performance analysis (instructional requirements), and context analysis (constraints, resources, and learner characteristics" (Seels & Glasgow, 1998, p. 13). The second project management phase encompasses design, development, and formative evaluation. Double-ended arrows connecting each of the six steps with a central oval labeled "Feedback and Interaction" illustrate this phase's interactive and dynamic nature. Completion of phase two occurs after obtaining satisfactory results from the formative evaluation. Phase three, implementation and evaluation, includes preparing training materials and offering training for users, creating support structures, summatively evaluating the instruction, and disseminating information about the project.

The ISD model 2 works for developers of products and lessons with the expectation the results will be disseminated for use by others. The somewhat unique features of the model are its emphasis on management and on early and continuing attention to diffusion of the results.

9   The Kemp Model

The current version of this popular ID model was initially created by Kemp and adapted by Kemp, Morrison and Ross in 1994. In its eighth edition, the book's authors include Gary R. Morrison, Steven M. Ross, Jennifer R. Morrison, and Howard K. Kalman, but the essential influence of Kemp remains obvious. The model remains unchanged, and the latest edition updates the context to reflect current research and trends, including new sections in each chapter to address completing each phase with fewer resources or time than optimal.

Past updates to this model include design considerations for technology-based instruction, classifying digital instruction modes into five groups: drill-and-practice, tutorials, simulations, games, and hypermedia. The guidance also addresses the affordances of each type of instruction along with detailing design considerations for both individualized and group-based instruction, making it an excellent model for instructional design projects with specialized taxonomy elements.

Morrison et al. (2019) present an instructional development model (Figure 17) focusing on curriculum planning. Morrison et al. approach instruction from

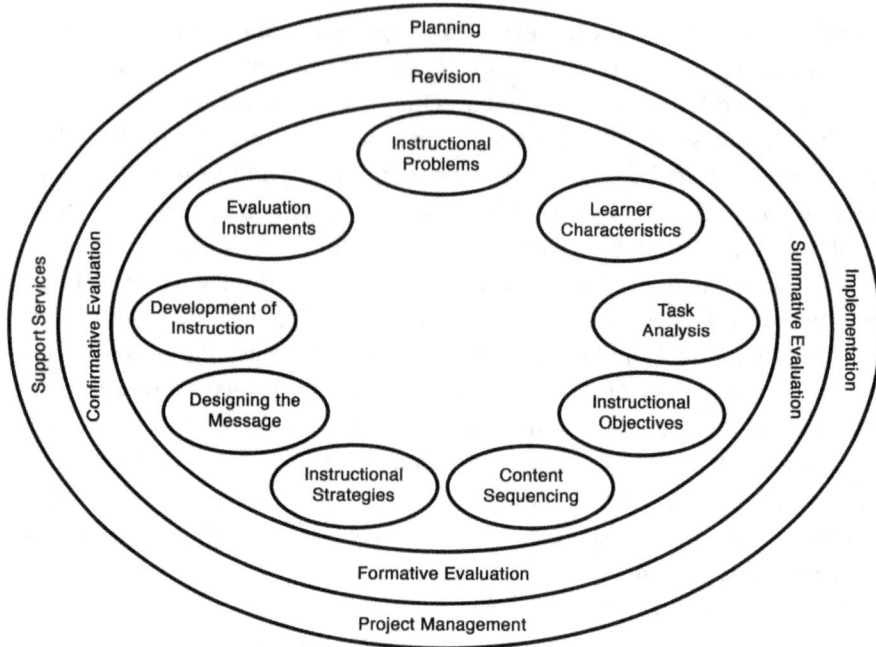

FIGURE 17   The Kemp model (from Morrison, Ross, Morrison, & Kalman, 2019, p. 3)

the perspective of the learner rather than from the content and contrast ID with traditional design practice by asking the following six questions:
– What level of readiness do individual students need for accomplishing the objectives?
– What instructional strategies are most appropriate in terms of objectives and learner characteristics?
– What technology or other resources are most suitable?
– What support is needed for successful learning?
– How is achievement of the objectives measured?
– What revisions are necessary if a tryout of the program does not match expectations (p. 9)?

Based on how various individuals would approach designing a course, Morrison et al. identify four fundamental planning elements for systematic instructional planning that are represented by answers to the following questions:
– For whom is the program developed? (learners)
– What do you want the learners or trainees to learn or demonstrate? (objectives)
– How is the subject content or skill best learned? (methods)
– How do you determine the extent to which learning is achieved? (evaluation)

The entirety of the Kemp model includes the interrelated elements of the framework as they relate to additional components and ongoing processes that continue throughout the life of an instructional design project, as illustrated by the outer ovals in Figure 17.

The Kemp model communicates the belief that ID is a continuous cycle with revision as an ongoing activity associated with all the other elements. The authors feel the designer can start anywhere and proceed in any order, espousing a general system view of development. In other words, all parts are interdependent and may be performed independently or simultaneously as appropriate. Although the Kemp model indicates the developer can start anywhere, the authors present a conventional framework in the narrative, starting with topics—tasks and purposes.

The classroom orientation of the model is apparent through their choice of the words, "topics" and "subject content," for determining what will be taught. However, both K-12 and business and industry instructors can readily identify with these words. The emphasis on subject matter content, goals and purposes, and selection of resources makes it attractive to higher education instructional designers, especially with design considerations for technology-based instruction. Further, project management guidance gives the model a modern. This model is one of the few that continues to be modified over time.

10   The Layers-of-Necessity Model

Tessmer and Wedman (1990) developed the Layers-of-Necessity model as an answer to the criticism that other ID models were too complex, creating unrealistic expectations and requiring unrealistic resources. Instead, the authors argued for an approach that accepts an evolutionary approach, recognizing "that instruction evolves over time rather than emerges fully developed" (p. 77). The resulting model (Figure 18) assumes that designers should choose a layer of design and related development activities based on the time and resources available, matching the layer to the project's necessities.

The simplicity of the Layers-of-Necessity model respects the complexities of learning design while attending to the constraints that often supersede other design decisions. For example, the authors note that learning design projects contain inherent limitations, such as time and resources. When these constraints are severe, the authors recommend working on the simplest layer of the project. Then, as time allows or resources become available or change, the designer can revisit the layer to incorporate additional design preferences or create additional layers, adding to the project's complexity.

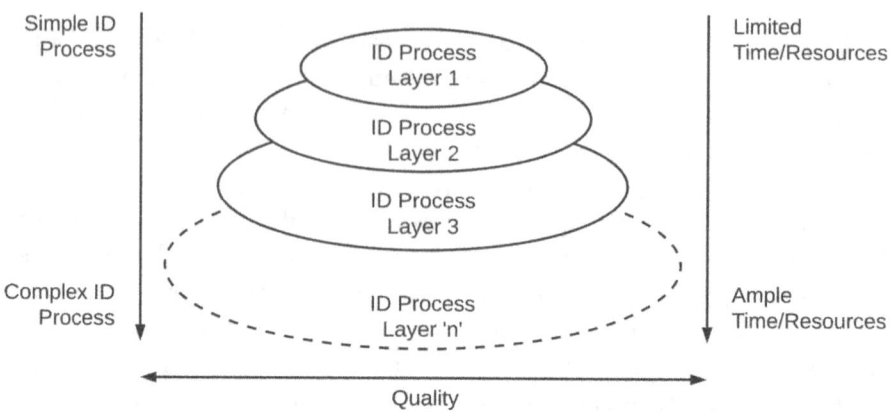

FIGURE 18 The Layers-of-Necessity model (from Tessmer & Wedman, 1990, p. 79)

Tessmer and Wedman differentiate the Layers-of-Necessity model in five ways. First, the authors view task enhancement as the most important aspect of progressing through the ID process. Where most models dictate a sequential flow and emphasize closing out a phase before moving on to the next, Layers-of-Necessity suggests an iterative design process. Second, the authors feel that principles of selection and implementation take precedent over fixed procedures. In other words, designers need to select which ID activities are necessary to meet the project guidelines, and to what complexity. Third, the authors view layers as merged stages that are more important than discrete tasks. This perspective allows designers to focus attention on essential aspects of the design. Fourth, the Layers-of-Necessity model facilitates a comprehensive perspective, allowing designers to minimize or omit components to the benefit of the learning product. Lastly, Tessmer and Wedman argue against traditional models' resource-intensive approaches, favoring the efficiency-based approach found in Layers-of-Necessity.

The practical approach of the Layers-of-Necessity model works well as a supplement to other ID models or stand on its own as a design paradigm. In learning design contexts where the learning space unexpectedly changes during delivery or other design factors or elements require adjusting prior to project completion, the model represents a flexible approach to re-contextualizing. However, the model's reliance on existing familiarity with common ID competencies also makes it better suited for intermediate to advanced IDs in practice.

11   The Pebble in the Pond Model

As a result of his work identifying first principles of instruction, Merrill has contributed to one of the most widely discussed and used instructional design

THE MODELS

models in the past decade. Merrill's (2009) systematic review of instructional design theories, models, and research concluded that well-designed instruction possesses five core principles indicative of its effectiveness, efficiency, and engagement. These five principles are demonstration, application, task-centered, activation, and integration. Merrill asserts that learning is promoted when learners observe a demonstration, apply the new knowledge, engage in a task-centered instructional strategy, activate relevant prior knowledge, and integrate new knowledge into their everyday activities.

Initially published in 2009, Merrill's (2002, 2020) Pebble in the Pond development model (Figure 19) is based upon these first principles of instruction and considers each principle within a series of expanding activities. However, Merrill believes the Pebble in the Pond to be a content-centered modification that should be used in conjunction with traditional instructional systems design. For this reason, we consider Merrill's model a product-oriented model. The revised edition focuses more on contextual details around ID practices than changes to the model or its primary events.

With respect to the integrative nature of Merrill's first principles of instruction and Pebble in the Pond development, designers must make a series of decisions and complete the correlated actions. As Merrill (2020) states:

> The metaphor is an environmental pond in which instruction is to occur. The pebble is a problem that learners need to be able to solve in the context of the pond. The problem, the pebble thrown into the instructional pond, is the trigger for the instructional design process. The instructional event comprising the first ripple is selecting a class of problems to be solved by the learners. The second ripple is defining the progression of problem instances. The third ripple is designing instructional strategies

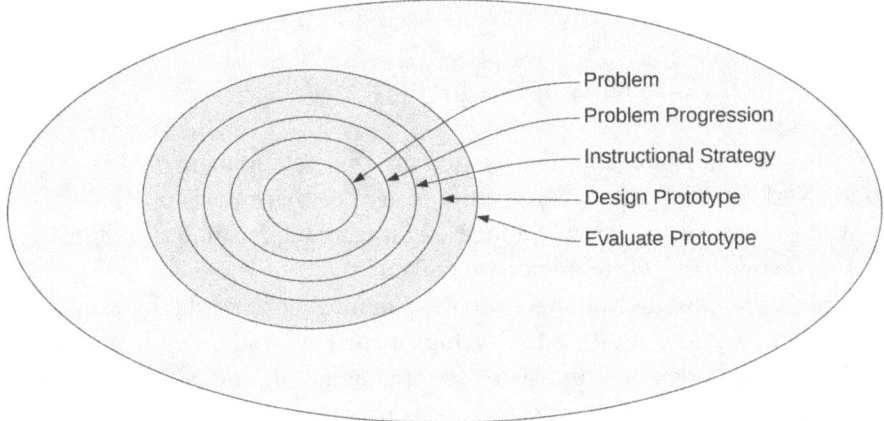

FIGURE 19   The Pebble in the Pond model (from Merrill, 2020, p. 166)

for e3 instruction for each problem instance in the progression. The fourth ripple is designing a functional prototype of the instruction. The fifth ripple is evaluating and revising the prototype. (p. 166)

Merrill contextualizes the first principles with examples of generalizable skills with procedures. Examples explain generalizable skills categorized as concept classification (kinds-of), procedural (how-to), or predicting consequences (what-happens) to illustrate potential strategies. Merrill notes that failure to provide sufficient demonstration often plagues instruction, thus the need for categorizing and consistency when presenting information. Further, using consistent demonstration, designers can provide activities that allow for consistent application of the skill(s) to be learned.

At this point in the process, Merrill points out that designing task-centered strategies is not the same as problem-based instructional strategies. The primary difference is that task-centered instructional strategies are a form of direct instruction placed within the context of authentic, real-world tasks. An efficiently structured task-centered strategy provides a framework within which learners can activate prior knowledge and integrate this with newly acquired skills. Reflection, peer critiques, personal use, and public demonstration each contribute effectively to integrating new knowledge and skills into everyday activities. Once fully planned, combining content and instructional strategies in the design process takes the designer through to the production "ripple" of the model.

The Pebble in the Pond model is unique in that Merrill intends for the process to fit within other instructional design processes instead of standing alone. However, the integration of Merrill's first principles of instruction within the model allows for the possibility of independent use. As training and instructional needs become increasingly diverse, the model is well suited for use in a variety of elements encountered in learning contexts.

12   The Understanding by Design (UbD) Model

Wiggins and McTigue (2005) developed the Understanding by Design (UbD) framework, also known as "backwards design" or "backwards planning," as a way for educators to plan while focused on teaching for understanding. The authors based UbD on eight fundamental tenets:
- UbD is a way to think about curricular planning, not a rigid program
- The primary goal of UBD is to develop and deepen student understanding
- UbD breaks down and translates content standards and goals into Stage 1 elements and appropriate Stage 2 assessments

- Understanding is revealed when students transfer learning into authentic performance
- Effective curriculum is planned backwards from long-term desired results through a three-stage process
- Teachers are coaches of understanding whose focus is to ensure learning
- Units and curriculum must be regularly reviewed against design standards to enhance quality and effectiveness
- UbD is a continuous improvement approach to achievement

The authors designed UbD with three stages. Stage 1 includes identifying desired results. In this stage, educators ask what long-term transfer goals to target, what meanings students should make, what essential questions will students consider, what knowledge and skill will students acquire, and what established goals to target. In Stage 2, designers determine acceptable evidence by asking what performances and products will reveal meaningful transfer, what criteria will determine Stage 1 results, and if all assessments align with Stage 1 elements. Finally, the actual planning of learning experiences and instruction occurs in Stage 3. In this stage, designers identify activities, experiences, and lessons to achieve Stage 1 results and Stage 2 assessments. Other questions asked during Stage 2 include how the learning plan helped students achieve transfer with increasing independence, how to monitor progress, how to sequence the unit and offer differentiation for all learners, and how learning events aligned with Stage 1 goals and Stage 2 assessments.

Wiggins and McTighe prescribe sketching out unit ideas in a table divided into three columns (one for each of the three stages). In the first column, the designer should write the desired result for learners. Necessary evidence required to prove the learned knowledge or skills goes in the second column. Finally, the designer records learning events that would produce the evidence needed in the third column. This practice facilitates alignment between the three stages for each identified outcome.

As a cautionary warning, the authors also detail the "twin sins of typical unit planning" (pp. 8–9). The first sin, labeled as activity-oriented teaching, occurs more often at the elementary and middle school level. In other words, designers plan activities to be more engaging and kid-friendly without considering how to create coherent, focused, and generative learning. The second sin, more common at the secondary and post-secondary level, involves working through a specific resource without consideration for engaging activities. In the latter case, resources become the focus of instruction instead of learning outcomes that use the resource. UbD can fit any learning space, but generally appears in the literature relating to in-person instruction.

CHAPTER 5

Discussion

The literature is replete with instructional design models, many claiming to be unique and deserving of attention. However, while there are hundreds of models, until recently, there have been only a few significant distinctions among them. Many of the models are simply restatements of earlier models by other authors, often using somewhat different terminology. Further, typical journal articles briefly describe the major steps in an ID model and perhaps how to perform them. Books on the topic (e.g., Dick et al., 2015; Smith & Ragan, 2005) are more likely to provide extensive guidance on applying the models, including contextual considerations. Thus, this survey covers a representative sample of ID models and presents a fully revised taxonomy to evaluate any ID model within the context of the learning space and related factors and elements.

Authors often assume their models are worthwhile in almost all instances but present no evidence to substantiate their positions. Moreover, the small amount of literature describing applied use or testing of the models is disconcerting. Therefore, we encourage instructional design scholars, especially those undertaking design-based research, to clearly articulate the ID model(s) applied and the impact of this decision on their study. Such attention would effectively close the gap in providing secondary data for ID model validation. An exploratory version of such an exercise might refer to the useful compilation of short case studies by (Ertmer et al., 2019), systematically exploring suitability with specific ID models.

1   Scholarly Contributions

We also encourage instructional design scholars to consider rigorous validation procedures when revising or creating new ID models. Such validation requires a precise description of the model elements followed by systematic data collection concerning their application and the impact of the resulting instruction. Detailed descriptions will also address discrepant or negative data, aiding discussion and revisions. If the model has validity, repeated trials under such conditions will result in specifications regarding the conditions under which the model fits. It is safe to say none of the models currently available in the literature has experienced such rigorous scrutiny. Most authors completely ignore the issue of what conditions should be present if one plans to use their models. For a complete discussion of procedures for validating a model, we defer to (Rubinstein, 1975) chapter on models and modeling.

How should the responsible ID professional respond to the plethora of ID models? First, we suggest that designers acquire a working knowledge of several models, gaining confidence in how they represent all three taxonomy categories. Then, when encountering new and revised models, you can compare these to familiar models and the taxonomy. Such an acumen will also aid designers with adopting client-provided or preferred models. Second, we recommend having a repertoire of example models to present to clients and stakeholders with varying levels of detail. This approach provides a baseline introduction to later expanded, providing additional detail for uninformed clients as they become more experienced. Third, instructional designers should be prepared to select an appropriate model rather than forcing the situation to fit the model when facing a range of conditions. Dills and Romiszowski (1997) state this position best, "instructional design is, and always will be, (emphasis added) a practice based on multiple paradigms" (p. XII). We believe all competent professional developers should have several models in their tool bags and use the right one, perhaps with modification for the right job.

2 Trends & Forecasting

Looking back over the past decade, we see significant trends continuing momentum after several decades of little change in the underlying structure of the ID process and its accompanying models. Although some might argue that renewed interest in constructivism (an old idea rediscovered) forms the basis for this trend, we believe the challenges encountered during rapid transitions to remote teaching (see Hodges et al., 2020) and continued advancements in technology contribute more significantly. For example, rapid prototyping models and models exhibiting more flexibility, such as Layers-of-Necessity, pose more value for designers with uncertain parameters. The emergence and popularity of these models closely parallel the creation of tools to facilitate quick and inexpensive content development and modification of prototypes not previously possible. Instructional designers often appreciate the power of prototypes to generate creative thinking and test the feasibility of design ideas. However, until tools became available, most developers were forced to use the "design by analysis" approach common among classic ID models.

Other forces influencing how we think about the ID process include performance support systems, knowledge management, and concurrent engineering. Most of the interest in performance support to date occurs in occupational job support, but this idea also extends to formal learning environments. There are at least two issues here. One issue is, *how can ID contribute to the design of performance support systems?* The second issue is, *how do we design training to complement performance support since many will require at least some prior or concurrent knowledge and skill development?* There are similar issues related to knowledge management. Effective knowledge management systems require much more than simply organizing and making large quantities of data available to users. Data management is not instruction. Although most interest in knowledge management appears in the commercial sector, we believe it also has implications for designing classroom and independent learning environments. Similarly, as concurrent engineering becomes more common, instructional designers must be part of development teams if they hope to be central to the primary business of corporations and large social services agencies. Being an initial member of a cross-disciplinary team creating a new product or process will require ID models and practices beyond traditional practice.

Educational technologies experienced unprecedented growth in the last decade due to increased demand and new challenges. These tools range from the straightforward, such as collaborative browser-based whiteboards, to the very complex, such as virtual reality-based meeting spaces. Additionally, ID professionals often create templates and tools to support their work and that of others as they license or openly share these aids through networked communities. Goodyear (2013) and van den Akker et al. (1999) provide thorough descriptions of such tools and practices from a traditional perspective. For a contemporary view of this practice in K-12 settings, see Shelton and Archambault (2019). Further, software and applications to support automating the ID process, including development and evaluation, are increasing, aided by a rise in venture capital funding and entrepreneurial competitions (e.g., *Futures Forum on Learning, Global EdTech Startups Awards, Panasci Competition*, etc.). Integrating traditional ID processes with artificial intelligence-enhanced tools will play an expanded role over the next decade.

ID practices will continue to evolve, but the future remains unclear for ID models themselves. After a relatively long period of slow evolution of ID practice, rapid advancements and investments in technology are driving changes in every sector using instructional design. Additionally, the need to focus on non-tangible aspects of the learner, such as culture, or use collaborative tools and a workforce shift to accommodate distributed teams change the dynamics of necessary ID competencies. For example, ATD Research (2015) previously found cultural context and integrating technology options ranked low(er) in required competencies. A repeat of this survey today would likely yield a very different result. In any case, the potential impact on ID models is yet to be determined.

3 Conclusion

Instructional designers increase their potential for success when the applied model matches the learning context. However, instructional designers should consider specific contextual elements that require additional considerations, such as flexibility to manage the scope of practice, accommodations for desired learning strategies, and consideration of various reality traits. Further, people who employ ID models should explore the shifting landscape of instructional design competencies required to successfully implement learning designs, comparing the last discussion from Richey et al. (2001) to a more recent summary from Martin and Ritzhaupt (2021). Finally, this survey of ID models should assist you in creating a personal mental model to aid in adopting or adapting existing models or when encountering a new model. Remember, the goal of any instructional design model is to increase the potential for fidelity between the learning context and the desired outcomes.

References

Andrews, D. H., & Goodson, L. A. (1980). A comparative analysis of models of instructional design. *Journal of Instructional Development, 3*(4), 2–16. https://doi.org/10.1007/BF02904348

Ashby, W. R. (1957). *An introduction to cybernetics.* Chapman & Hall. http://pcp.vub.ac.be/books/IntroCyb.pdf

Association for Educational Communications and Technology. (1977). *Educational technology definition and glossary of terms.* Association for Educational Communications and Technology.

ATD Research. (2015). *Skills, challenges, and trends in instructional design.* https://www.td.org/Publications/Research-Reports/2015/Skills-Challenges-and-Trends-in-Instructional-Design

Barson, J. (1967). *Instructional systems development: A demonstration and evaluation project: Final report.* U.S. Department of Health, Education and Welfare. https://eric.ed.gov/?id=ED020673

Beck, K., Beedle, M., van Bennekum, A., Cockburn, A., Cunningham, W., Fowler, M., Grenning, J., Highsmith, J., Hunt, A., Jeffries, R., Kern, J., Marick, B., Martin, R. C., Mellor, S., Schwaber, K., Sutherland, J., & Thomas, D. (2001). *Manifesto for Agile software development.* http://agilemanifesto.org/

Beckschi, P., & Doty, M. (2000). Instructional systems design: A little bit of ADDIEtude, please. In G. M. Piskurich, P. Beckschi, & B. Hall (Eds.), *The ASTD handbook of training design and delivery* (pp. 28–41). McGraw-Hill.

Berkowitz, M., & O'Neil, H. F., Jr. (1979). *An annotated bibliography for instructional systems development.* http://hdl.handle.net/2027/osu.32435006939474

Berrett, D. (2016, February 29). Instructional design: Demand grows for a new breed of academic. *The Chronicle of Higher Education.* https://www.chronicle.com/article/instructional-design/

Branch, R. M. (1997). Perceptions of instructional design process models. In R. E. Griffin, D. G. Beauchamp, J. M. Hunter, & C. B. Schiffman (Eds.), *VisionQuest: Journeys toward visual literacy: Selected readings from the annual conference of the International Visual Literacy Association* (pp. 429–433). https://eric.ed.gov/?id=ED417056

Branch, R. M. (1999). Instructional design: A conceptual parallel processor for navigating learning space. In J. van den Akker, R. M. Branch, K. L. Gustafson, N. M. Nieveen, & T. Plomp (Eds.), *Design approaches and tools in education and training* (pp. 145–154). Springer. https://doi.org/10.1007/978-94-011-4255-7_12

Branch, R. M. (2017). Characteristics of foundational instructional design models. In R. A. Reiser & J. v. Dempsey (Eds.), *Trends and issues in instructional design and technology* (4th ed., pp. 23–30). Pearson.

Branch, R. M., & Dousay, T. A. (2015). *Survey of instructional design models* (5th ed.). Association for Educational Communications & Technology. https://aect.org/survey_of_instructional_design.php

Branch, R. M., Mané, C. E., & Shin, M. Y. (2018). Effect of graphic element type on visual perceptions of curvilinear and rectilinear flow diagrams. *Journal of Visual Literacy, 37*(2), 119–136. https://doi.org/10.1080/1051144X.2018.1493249

Branson, R. K., Rayner, G. T., Cox, L., Furman, J. P., & King, F. J. (1975). *Interservice procedures for instructional systems development. Executive summary and model*. National Technical Information Service. https://eric.ed.gov/?id=ED164745

Cennamo, K. S., & Kalk, D. (2019). *Real world instructional design: An iterative approach to designing learning experiences* (2nd ed.). Routledge.

Decherney, P., & Lavender, C. (2020, April 24). The hottest job in higher education: Instructional designer. *Inside Higher Ed*. https://www.insidehighered.com/digital-learning/blogs/education-time-corona/hottest-job-higher-education-instructional-designer

Dick, W., Carey, L., & Carey, J. O. (2015). *The systematic design of instruction* (8th ed.). Pearson.

Dills, C. R., & Romiszowski, A. J. (Eds.). (1997). *Instructional development paradigms*. Educational Technology Publications.

Edmonds, G. S., Branch, R. C., & Mukherjee, P. (1994). A conceptual framework for comparing instructional design models. *Educational Technology Research and Development, 42*(4), 55–72. https://doi.org/10.1007/BF02298055

Ely, D. P. (1973). Defining the field of educational technology. *Audiovisual Instruction, 8*(3), 52–53.

Ely, D. P. (1983). The definition of educational technology: An emerging stability. *Educational Considerations, 10*(2), 1–4. https://doi.org/10.4148/0146-9282.1793

Ertmer, P. A., Quinn, J. A., & Glazewski, K. D. (2019). *The ID casebook: Case studies in instructional design* (5th ed.). Routledge. https://doi.org/10.4324/9781315148083

Gagné, R. M., Wager, W. W., Golas, K. C., & Keller, J. M. (2004). *Principles of instructional design* (5th ed.). Cengage Learning.

Gerlach, V. S., & Ely, D. P. (1980). *Teaching and media: A systematic approach* (2nd ed.). Prentice-Hall.

Gentry, C. G. (1994). *Introduction to instructional development: Process and technique*. Wadsworth Publishing Company.

Goodyear, P. (1997). Instructional design environments: Methods and tools for the design of complex instructional systems. In S. Dijkstra, N. M. Seel, F. Schott, & R. D. Tennyson (Eds.), *Instructional design international perspectives: Volume 2 Solving Instructional Design Problems* (pp. 83–111). Lawrence Erlbaum Associates, Publishers. https://doi.org/10.4324/9781315044743-13

Gordon, J., & Zemke, R. (2000). The attack on ISD. *Training, 37*(4), 43–53.

References

Greer, M. (1992). *ID project management: Tools and techniques for instructional designers and developers*. Educational Technology Publications.

Gustafson, K. L. (1981). *Survey of instructional development models* (1st ed.). Syracuse University.

Gustafson, K. L. (1991). *Survey of instructional development models* (2nd ed.). ERIC Clearinghouse on Information Resources.

Gustafson, K. L., & Branch, R. M. (1997). *Survey of instructional development models* (3rd ed.). Syracuse University.

Gustafson, K. L., & Branch, R. M. (2002). *Survey of instructional development models* (4th ed.). Syracuse University.

Hamreus, D. G. (1967). The systems approach to instructional development. In *The contribution of behavioral science to instructional technology* (pp. I1–I59). Oregon State System of Higher Education, Teaching Research Division.

Heinich, R., Molenda, M., & Russell, J. D. (1981). *Instructional media and the new technologies of instruction*. John Wiley & Sons.

Hodges, C., Moore, S., Lockee, B., Trust, T., & Bond, A. (2020, March 27). The difference between emergency remote teaching and online learning. *EDUCASE Review*. https://er.educause.edu/articles/2020/3/the-difference-between-emergency-remote-teaching-and-online-learning

Markle, S. M. (1964). *Good frames and bad: A grammar of frame writing* (2nd ed.). John Wiley & Sons.

Markle, S. M. (1978). *Designs for instructional designers*. Stipes Publishing Co.

Martin, F., & Ritzhaupt, A. D. (2021). Standards and competencies for instructional design and technology professionals. In J. K. McDonald & R. E. West (Eds.), *Design for learning: Principles, processes, and praxis* (pp. 233–242). EdTech Books. https://edtechbooks.org/id

Merrill, M. D. (2002). A pebble-in-the-pond model for instructional design. *Performance Improvement, 41*(7), 41–46. https://doi.org/10.1002/pfi.4140410709

Merrill, M. D. (2009). First principles of instruction. In C. M. Reigeluth & A. A. Carr-Chellman (Eds.), *Instructional design theories and models: Building a common knowledge base: Vol. III* (Issue 3, pp. 43–59). Routledge Publishers. https://aect.org/firstprinciples.php

Merrill, M. D. (2020). *First principles of instruction* (rev. ed.). Association for Educational Communications & Technology.

Moore, S. (2021). The design models we have are not the design models we need. *Journal of Applied Instructional Design, 10*(4), 1–10. https://doi.org/10.51869/104/smo

Morrison, G. R., Ross, S. M., Morrison, J. R., & Kalman, H. K. (2019). *Designing effective instruction* (8th ed.). Wiley.

National Special Media Institute. (1971). *What is an IDI?* Michigan State University.

Reiser, R. A. (2018). A history of instructional design and technology. In R. A. Reiser & J. v. Dempsey (Eds.), *Trends and issues in instructional design and technology* (4th ed., pp. 8–22). Pearson.

Richey, R. C., Fields, D. C., & Foxon, M. (2001). *Instructional design competencies: The standards* (3rd ed.). ERIC Clearinghouse on Information & Technology. https://eric.ed.gov/?id=ED453803

Ritzhaupt, A. D., Kumar, S., & Martin, F. (2021). The competencies for instructional designers in higher education. In J. Stefaniak, S. Conklin, B. Oyarzun, & R. M. Reese (Eds.), *A practitioner's guide to instructional design in higher education*. EdTech Books. https://edtechbooks.org/id_highered/the_competencies_for

Rubinstein, M. F. (1975). *Patterns of problem solving*. Prentice-Hall.

Salisbury, D. F. (1989). What should instructional designers know about general systems theory? *Educational Technology, 29*(8), 42–45.

Seel, N. M. (1997). Models of instructional design: Introduction and overview. In R. D. Tennyson, F. Schott, N. M. Seel, & S. Dijkstra (Eds.), *Instructional design: International perspectives* (Vol. 1, pp. 355–360). Routledge.

Seels, B., & Glasgow, Z. (1997). *Making instructional design decisions*. Prentice-Hall.

Seels, B., & Richey, R. C. (1994). *Instructional technology: The definitions and domains of the field*. Association for Educational Communications and Technology.

Shelton, C. C., & Archambault, L. M. (2019). Who are online teacherpreneurs and what do they do? A survey of content creators on TeachersPayTeachers.com. *Journal of Research on Technology in Education, 51*(4), 398–414. https://doi.org/10.1080/15391523.2019.1666757

Silvern, L. C. (1965). *Basic analysis*. Education and Training Consultants Company.

Smith, P. L., & Ragan, T. J. (2005). *Instructional design* (3rd ed.). John Wiley and Sons.

Stamas, S. T. (1972). *A descriptive study of a synthesized model, reporting its effectiveness, efficiency, and cognitive and affective influence of the development process on a client*. Michigan State University. https://d.lib.msu.edu/etd/42365

Tessmer, M., & Wedman, J. F. (1990). A Layers-of-Necessity instructional development model. *Educational Technology Research & Development, 38*(2), 77–85. https://doi.org/10.1007/BF02298271

Twelker, P. A., Urbach, F. D., & Buck, J. E. (1972). *The systematic development of instruction: An overview and basic guide to the literature*. ERIC Clearinghouse on Educational Media and Technology.

van den Akker, J., Branch, R. M., Gustafson, K. L., Nieveen, N. M., & Plomp, T. (1999). *Design approaches and tools in education and training*. Springer. https://doi.org/10.1007/978-94-011-4255-7

van Merriënboer, J. J. G., & Kirschner, P. A. (2007). *Ten steps to complex learning: A systematic approach to four-component instructional design*. Lawrence Erlbaum Associates.

Wiggins, G. P., & McTigue, J. (2005). *Understanding by design* (1st ed.). ACSD College Textbook Series.

You, Y. (1993). What can we learn from chaos theory? An alternative approach to instructional systems design. *Educational Technology Research and Development*, *41*(3), 17–32. https://doi.org/10.1007/BF02297355

Young, P. A. (2008). The culture based model: Constructing a model of culture. *Educational Technology & Society*, *11*(2), 107–118.

Zemke, R., & Kramlinger, T. (1982). *Figuring things out: A trainer's guide to needs and task analysis*. Addison-Wesley Publishing Company.

Annotated Bibliography

Adnan, N. H., & Ritzhaupt, A. D. (2018). Software engineering design principles applied to instructional design: What can we learn from our sister discipline? *TechTrends, 62*(1), 77–94. https://doi.org/10.1007/s11528-017-0238-5

Poor instructional design accounts for the failure of many instructional design initiatives. Unfortunately, current instructional design models provide little insight into design processes for creating e-learning instructional solutions. Given the similarities between the fields of instructional design and software engineering, instructional designers could employ the ideas and techniques employed in software engineering to improve their design solutions.

Baturay, M. H. (2008). Characteristics of basic instructional design models. *Ekev Akademi Dergisi, 12*(34), 471–482

An instructional design indicates the existing plan and processes for any instruction regardless of the field of study. It works as a guide indicating how to implement instruction. The basic routine of instructional design includes and follows the stages of analysis, design, development, implementation, and evaluation. Although this is common among almost all instructional design models, they have minor differences.

Cennamo, K. S. (2003). Design as knowledge construction. *Computers in the Schools, 20*(4), 13–35. https://doi.org/10.1300/J025v20n04_03

Emerging from the analysis and reflection on the process of designing materials for constructivist learning environments, the author presents the *Layers of Negotiation* model of instructional design. The author offers insights on this model, which evolved in a spiral fashion in stages of analysis, design, development, and evaluation.

Dickey, M. D. (2006). Girl gamers: The controversy of girl games and the relevance of female-oriented game design for instructional design. *British Journal of Educational Technology, 37*(5), 785–793. https://doi.org/10.1111/j.1467-8535.2006.00561.x

This article discusses the emergence of girl games and the design of constructivist learning environments from a female-oriented game design perspective. The author presents an overview of digital games and gender, an outline of girl games and 'pink' software, a discussion of the controversy of girl games, and a review and discussion of the research and implications of female-oriented game design for instructional design.

Göksu, I., Özcan, K. V., Cakir, R., & Göktas, Y. (2017). Content analysis of research trends in instructional design models: 1999–2014. *Journal of Learning Design, 10*(2), 85. https://doi.org/10.5204/jld.v10i2.288

The researchers examined 113 studies on instructional design models by applying content analysis. Data included articles published in 44 international Social Science Citation Index (SSCI) and Science Citation Index (SCI) journals. Instructional design model analysis considered journal of publication, preferred model, study location, research method, data collection tool, data analysis method, sampling interval, and field of application. The analysis concludes that systems-based models are currently the most common.

Güney, Z. (2019). Four-Component Instructional Design (4C/ID) model approach for teaching programming skills. *International Journal of Progressive Education, 15*(4), 142–156. https://doi.org/10.29329/ijpe.2019.203.11

The author designed and tested an instructional design model (4C/ID) activity, adapting the principles of the model for teaching technical skills. Implications include using the activity to teach the importance of instructional and technological stages by combining and supporting other multimedia project design, development, and evaluation models.

Hoogveld, A. W. M. M., Paas, F., Jochems, W. M. G. G., & van Merriënboer, J. J. G. G. (2002). Exploring teachers' instructional design practices from a systems design perspective. *Instructional Science, 30*(4), 291–305. https://doi.org/10.1023/A:1016081812908

This exploratory analysis conducted in the Netherlands included the design activities of ten teacher trainers in response to higher education vocational curriculum changes. The authors compare the design practices with an instructional systems design (ISD) approach, discussing how the trainers failed to address problem analysis and evaluation. The study implications note a negative impact on innovative teacher roles.

Jonassen, D. H. (2006). On the role of concepts in learning and instructional design. *Educational Technology Research and Development, 54*(2), 177–196. https://doi.org/10.1007/s11423-006-8253-9

This article defines concepts and describes their importance to learning and instruction. The author discusses the importance of conceptual change, implications for concept learning, a need for research assessing conceptual change, and the role of assessing patterns of concepts and concepts-in-use.

Khodabandelou, R., & Samah, S. A. A. (2012). Instructional design models for online instruction: From the perspective of Iranian higher education. *Procedia – Social and Behavioral Sciences, 67*, 545–552. https://doi.org/10.1016/j.sbspro.2012.11.359

This study sought to understand how ID models are used to design and develop online instruction, positing which elements are most necessary. The researchers employed a Delphi methodology, finding four most commonly used models and three vital elements.

Koper, R., Giesbers, B., van Rosmalen, P., Sloep, P., van Bruggen, J., Tattersall, C., Vogten, H., & Brouns, F. (2005). A design model for lifelong learning networks. *Interactive Learning Environments*, *13*(1–2), 71–92. https://doi.org/10.1080/10494820500173656

This work discusses the implications of lifelong learning and conceptual demands of delivery, including learner-centered and learner-controlled instructional design models. The authors present a model for structuring Learning Networks, supported by software agents and open learning technology.

Magliaro, S. G., & Shambaugh, N. (2006). Student models of instructional design. *Educational Technology Research and Development*, *54*(1), 83–106. https://doi.org/10.1007/s11423-006-6498-y

This study analyzed 178 student-generated instructional design models to determine how graduate learners conceive mental models representative of practice. The researchers looked at ADDIE components and model structural characteristics. They found that students most often depict design, followed by program evaluation, needs assessment, development, and implementation.

Merrill, M. D. (2007). A task-centered instructional strategy. *Journal of Research on Technology in Education*, *40*(1), 5–22. https://doi.org/10.1080/15391523.2007.10782493

The author reviewed instructional design models and research on instructional design practices to identify the first principles of instruction. These principles, best implemented in the context of real-world tasks, prescribe a cycle of instruction consisting of activation, demonstration, application, and integration. A *Pebble-in-the-Pond* approach to instructional development prescribes a task-centered, content-first instructional design procedure to implement these first principles.

Schwartzman, R. (2006). Virtual group problem solving in the basic communication course: Lessons for online learning. *Journal of Instructional Psychology, 33*(1), 3–14.
http://www.learntechlib.org/p/98825/

The author addresses issues related to performance expectations in online learning for group problem-solving via threaded discussion boards. After four years of research in group problem solving in a higher education course, the author produces instructional guidelines to enrich the learning experience.

Song, H. D., Grabowski, B. L., Koszalka, T. A., & Harkness, W. L. (2006). Patterns of instructional-design factors prompting reflective thinking in middle-school and college level problem-based learning environments. *Instructional Science, 34*(1), 63–87.
https://doi.org/10.1007/s11251-005-6922-4

Researchers compared the patterns of middle school and college level learners in relation to reflexive thinking in problem-based learning (PBL) environments. Data analysis considered instructional design factors such as environment, teaching methods, scaffolding tools in conjunction with learners' age and developmental stage.

Soto, V. J. (2013). Which instructional design models are educators using to design virtual world instruction? *Journal of Online Learning and Teaching, 9*(3), 364

This study investigated instructional design (ID) models used to design virtual world instruction. Findings highlight common use of the ADDIE process and criticize a lack of flexibility and consideration for game design theory in current ID models.

Steed, R. (2014). A client-centered model of instructional design for psychoeducation interventions in occupational therapy. *Occupational Therapy in Mental Health, 30*(2), 126–143.
https://doi.org/10.1080/0164212X.2014.878536

Occupational therapists often use psychoeducational interventions in mental health settings. Recent systematic reviews have validated the efficacy of this approach. However, the occupational therapy literature on the instructional design process is scarce. The author uses behavioral, acquisitional, cognitive, and constructivist approaches to illustrate the design process in four vignettes.

> Tawfik, A. A., Rong, H., & Choi, I. (2015). Failing to learn: Towards a unified design approach for failure-based learning. *Educational Technology Research and Development, 63*(6), 975–994. https://doi.org/10.1007/s11423-015-9399-0

The authors note a lack of problem-solving task support for learners in many instructional systems. When present, these systems use instructional design models that progress the learner efficiently through the problem-solving process. The discussion explores how theoretical applications from various fields address failure as a means to engender learning and offers failure-based principles for learning systems design.

> van Berlo, M. P. W., Lowyck, J., & Schaafstal, A. (2007). Supporting the instructional design process for team training. *Computers in Human Behavior, 23*(3), 1145–1161. https://doi.org/10.1016/j.chb.2006.10.007

This work discusses instructional principles for team training in the military. The authors explore how to support instructional designers in analyzing team tasks, designing team training scenarios, and validating the quality of this support. The researchers tested guidelines in three experiments, finding evidence of improvements in the analysis and design phases.

> van Merriënboer, J. J. G. G., & Sweller, J. (2005). Cognitive load theory and complex learning: Recent developments and future directions. *Educational Psychology Review, 17*(2), 147–177. https://doi.org/10.1007/s10648-005-3951-0

This article reviews the outcomes of experimental studies in the area of Cognitive Load Theory (CLT) and instructional design connecting complex learning to real-life tasks. The authors explore instructional methods that address changes from simple to complex learning, short experiments to lengthy training programs, and preplanned instruction to adaptive eLearning.

> Verstegen, D. M. L., Barnard, Y. F., & Pilot, A. (2006). Which events can cause iteration in instructional design? An empirical study of the design process. *Instructional Science, 34*(6), 481–517. https://doi.org/10.1007/s11251-005-3346-0

Iteration involves returning to a design activity that the designer has already worked on before. This article discusses the implications of iteration during the instructional design process. Researchers introduced five events to trigger iterative actions. Findings note internal and external triggers of iteration but indicate no correlation in design quality and number of iterations.

> Wang, H.-C. (2007). Performing a course material enhancement process with asynchronous interactive online system. *Computers and Education, 48*(4), 567–581. https://doi.org/10.1016/j.compedu.2005.03.007

This article discusses the development of course materials for online learning systems, using modifications to course materials by students as design enhancements. According to the author, this type of student contribution to the design process guarantees improved course quality.

> Wiburg, K., Parra, J., Mucundanyi, G., Latorre, J., & Torres, R. C. (2017). Constructivist instructional design models applied to the design and development of digital mathematics game modules. *International Journal of Technology in Teaching and Learning, 13*(1), 1–15.

The authors report on part of a yearlong project investigating which instructional design (ID) models emphasize constructivism and how these models apply to the design of digital learning resources. The article reports on applying the questions in designing digital math game modules through a graduate-level course employing participatory class design.

Willis, J. (2000). The maturing of constructivist instructional design: Some basic principles that can guide practice. *Educational Technology, 40*(1), 5–16. http://www.jstor.org/stable/44428576

This article presents one of the first versions of an instructional design model based on constructivist learning theories and an interpretivist philosophy of science (Willis, 1995). The Recursive and Reflective Design and Development (R2D2) model was one of the first to outline an approach to creating instructional material based on constructivist theory. The author discusses guidelines for instructional design based on an interpretivist philosophy of science and constructivist theories of learning.

Wyrostek, W., & Downey, S. (2017). Compatibility of common instructional models with the DACUM process. *Adult Learning, 28*(2), 69–75. https://doi.org/10.1177/1045159516669702

Two researchers review prominent instructional design models and provide prescriptive guidance for selecting appropriate models given a project's Product Requirements, Resource Availability, and Philosophical Compatibility with *Developing A CurriculUM* (DACUM) procedures.

York, C. S., & Ertmer, P. A. (2016). Examining instructional design principles applied by experienced designers in practice. *Performance Improvement Quarterly, 29*(2), 169–192. https://doi.org/10.1002/piq.21220

The ongoing debate regarding the efficacy of teaching instructional design models to novice designers scrutinizes the argument that experienced instructional designers often use principles and adapted models when they engage in the instructional design problem-solving process. Using the Delphi technique, researchers identified a core set of guiding principles designers use in their practice.

www.ingramcontent.com/pod-product-compliance
Lightning Source LLC
Chambersburg PA
CBHW071934240426
43668CB00038B/1800